The Huguenots of New Bordeaux

Books by Bobby F. Edmonds

The Making of McCormick County
McCormick County Land of Cotton
Destiny of the Scots-Irish: A Family Saga
The Huguenots of New Bordeaux

The Huguenots of New Bordeaux

Bobby F. Edmonds

CEDAR HILL UNLTD.

The Huguenots of New Bordeaux

Copyright © 2005 by Bobby F. Edmonds

All rights reserved

First Edition

ISBN 978-0-9749976-3-6

Printed on acid free paper
in the United States of America
by
Sheridan Books, Inc.
100 North Staebler Road
Ann Arbor, MI 48103

Published by
Cedar Hill Unltd.
1000 Cedar Hill Road
McCormick, SC 29835
Email cedarhill@wctel.net

To the memory of

Sandra Delashaw Warden
(1939–2004)

Contents

Acknowledgments, ix

The Huguenot Cross, x

Introduction, 1

Chapter One, Religious Wars and Diaspora, 6

Chapter Two, The Pastor of the Desert, 16

Chapter Three, The Long Voyage, 24

Chapter Four, New Bordeaux Colony Founded, 43

Chapter Five, Assimilation, 74

Chapter Six, Hymnody and Psalmody, 86

Chapter Seven, Huguenots in the Novel, 99

Notes, 107

Bibliography, 111

Index, 113

Acknowledgments

When I was still a teenager, Dr. Nora Marshal Davis, a South Carolina history scholar of excellence, freely offered me her library for research. I had the good fortune of being a frequent visitor in her home in the little town of Troy for many years. The information gleaned from her extensive historical archives, especially heavy with Huguenot data, formed the foundation for this book. For her gracious contributions I am grateful.

I owe so much to Sandra Delashaw Warden, a top flight genealogist and historian. Her friendship and tremendous efforts have been monumental.

As always, I am indebted to Vicki M. Dorn and Karen L. Bowick at the *McCormick Messenger* for their day-to-day support and encouragement.

Dianne Purdy, Paul Brown, and Darby Furqueron at McCormick County Library never failed to cheerfully acquire books of vital importance to my research.

My gratitude I extend to accomplished artist James Bledsoe who created the cover illustration.

Thanks to Kathy DuLaney, J. P. Hester, and Anne C. Gibert for inspiration, to Phyllis Albert, my daughter Bonnie Brown, Todd Dillashaw, and Betty McCormick for technical support, and to Allen Stokes, South Caroliniana Library, and Lucy Ann Blanchard Singleton for archival assistance.

I am indebted to authors and historians from whose works I have cited.

I am grateful to my wife Kathryn for her abiding love and support.

THE HUGUENOT CROSS

Not long after the Revocation of the Edict of Nantes in 1685, the Huguenot Cross, or *the Cross of Languedoc*, came into general use among the Huguenots as confirmation of the wearer's faith.

The insignia consists of an open four-petal Lily of France - reminiscent of the Mother Country of France - in which each petal radiates outward in the shape of a "V" to form a Maltese Cross. The four petals signify the Four Gospels. Each petal, or arm, has at its outside periphery two rounded points at the corners. These rounded points are regarded as signifying the Eight Beatitudes.

The four petals are joined together by four fleur-de-lis, also reminiscent of the Mother Country of France. Each fleur-de-lis has three petals. The twelve petals of the four fleur-de-lis signify the Twelve Apostles.

An open space in the shape of a heart is formed between each fleur-de-lis and the arms of the two petals with which it is joined. This shape - a symbol of loyalty - suggests the seal of the great French Reformer, John Calvin.

A descending dove pendant representing the *Saint Esprit* or "Sainted Spirit" - the guide and counselor of the Church - is suspended from a ring of gold attached to the lower central petal.

The Huguenot Cross

"There is much that is admirable in the composition of the old Huguenots who settled the New Bordeaux neighborhood. They lived under the quiet of their own vine and fig tree and exemplified the domestic and social virtues that make the useful citizen and that render home sweet and attractive. Their names were synonymous of honestly and business integrity in every community in which known. There are people all over the country who esteem it a greater honor to have in their veins the blood of those old Huguenot pioneers of New Bordeaux than if it were the blood of dukes and of earls."

Homage to the Huguenots
by a great grandson of
Jean Bouchillon
The Press and Banner
July 3, 1895

Introduction

Indeed, no less than the New England Pilgrims, the descendants of *French Huguenot refugees* hold a certain pride - an unequivocal expression of what may be called *Huguenot esceptionalism*, utterly Calvinistic since in the eyes of Huguenot chroniclers, then and now, the migration was a selective one. In the eyes of the Huguenot descendants, and all of those who claim to have collectively inherited their "values," the Huguenots who fled France were the most devoted to and uncompromising in their faith, the most courageous, and the most enterprising. Certainly, their survival was heroic.

The colony of South Carolina stands out as having received the largest number of Huguenots. Of the fifteen locations in British North America where a significant number of refugees settled, seven of them were in South Carolina: Charleston, Goose Creek, Orange Quarter, French Santee, Saint John's Berkeley, and Purrysburgh (all in the low state), and New Bordeaux, the only one in up state South Carolina. All except New Bordeaux were settled during the first wave of the post-revocation era when South Carolina was in the hands of the Lords Proprietors.

The Huguenots of New Bordeaux

The New Bordeaux settlement, led by Pastor Jean Louis Gibert in present-day McCormick County, was not directly involved with the earlier Huguenot proprietary migration to South Carolina. Those refugees who migrated with Pastor Gibert in 1764 and with St. Pierre four years later did so under somewhat different circumstances. By that time, the Edict of Nantes had been revoked for more than eighty years, and their emigration was related to a new wave of religious persecution that affected certain areas of France. St. Pierre was taking a group of French and German Protestants to occupy lands granted them by the government at Cape Sable, in Nova Scotia and located in South Carolina only after having been driven by bad seas to land in Charleston. Both leaders were undoubted already familiar with the other Huguenot settlements in South Carolina.

The Huguenots were French Calvinists or French Reformed Protestants. Like the Scottish Presbyterians, they were followers of John Calvin (1509-64), brilliant French religious reformer. The Huguenot religion was distinctly Calvinist. It was John Calvin who wrote their Confession of Faith, adopted by the first Synod meeting in Paris in 1559. The Calvinist idea of Church government by a bench of elders, which came to be known as Presbyterian, was the form of government of the French Huguenot Church.

The Reformation in France in its principal and most durable form was essentially Calvinist. This final phase was well under way by the time of the catastrophic death of Henry II in July 1559, which led swiftly to the formation of the Huguenot faction.

The French Reformation had an extensive pre-Calvinist background, dating from approximately the second decade of the century. In a sense the Protestant Reformation might actually be said to have originated in France since, as early as 1512, after translating the Epistles of St. Paul, Lefevre d'Etaples derived from them the doctrine of justification *by faith alone*. This doctrine emphasized interior spirituality more than outward observance.

Introduction

Like Martin Luther and other religious thinkers of the sixteenth and seventeenth centuries, Calvin transformed the religious life of thousands who, with the invention of the printing press, were reading their own Bibles, in their own language, for the first time. They were questioning old teachings and beliefs. They were thinking for themselves.

John Calvin preached that salvation is by God's grace alone without any merit or worthiness on man's part. Whereas Martin Luther said that the Lord is not willing that any should perish and that man is himself to blame if he remains unbelieving and reprobate, Calvin was not satisfied with an agnostic answer to the question why some are saved and not others. He boldly stated that God made that choice in all eternity and cannot be questioned.

The result of the Reformation was the long conflict of religious wars served by the extreme Catholic policy aimed at exterminating the Huguenots.

The origin of the word "Huguenot" is not clear. Opinions include:

Heus quenaus, which in the Swiss patois signifies *seditious fellows*.

Heghenen or *Huguenen*, a Flemish word, which means *Puritans*, or *Cathari*.

One *Hugues*, a sacramentarian, is said to have given rise to the epithet.

Huguenote, the name given to common iron or earthenware pot for cooking, depicting the number of early Huguenots who perished in the flames.

Possibly the most widely accepted preference has the word derive from the Swiss German word *eidgnossen*, meaning *confederate* or *oath-bound* and referring to the inhabitants of Geneva in their struggle against the Duke of Savoy in the sixteenth century. *Eidgnossen* became *eyguenot* then *huguenot* (the opening "h" and the final "t" being silent).

In sixteenth century France in official records, the Huguenots were more often called *"members de la religion prétendue réformée."*

At any rate, being a Huguenot during the turbulent

times was dangerous. Indeed, before the Edict of Nantes if the Huguenot had his Bible in one hand, he need have his sword in the other.

In the 1560s, in the wake of the Calvinist reformation, the Huguenot population reached its all-time high watermark, some historians say perhaps 20 percent of the French population. In the seventeenth century, their numbers declined and leveled off at about 750,000, or 4 percent of the population. In the seventeenth century during the years preceding the Revocation, Huguenot churches were delegated primarily to the famed "Huguenot crescent or triangle," which extended from Alpine Dauphiny to Atlantic Aunis.

When they left France most Huguenots were destitute because the state had confiscated their possessions, the Catholic Church receiving part of the wealth. So it was not easy to flee. The French government reacted swiftly to what was happening, watching exit routes and searching ships. Pirates plundered ships leaving France, for there were bounties for capture of escapees. Huguenots who were found fleeing faced severe punishment. Making things harder, spies working within the communities tried to find out the names of those planning to fee and their routes.

Huguenot emigrants played an important cultural role in Europe and America. They used their newfound freedom to produce literature that helped to shape the philosophy of *the Enlightenment and ideas of tolerance*. For example, a French Huguenot translated the works of English philosopher John Locke, propagating the idea of natural rights. Other Huguenot writers emphasized the importance of freedom of conscience. The ideas developed that obedience to rulers is relative and could be ignored if they broke the contract that existed between them and the people.

The Huguenots received strength from a moving faith in God, and, amid the dark clouds of the turbulent era of the Reformation, they held tight to certain principles or ideals of the religious spirit - most especially religious freedom, intellectual freedom, and political freedom; they believed all three were actually intertwined.

Introduction

  Religious freedom took precedence over all other. Spiritual freedom coveted by the Huguenots reflected the Calvinist spirit of freedom of the soul, whereby religious liberty is the very essence of spiritual freedom guaranteeing the right to worship God according to the dictates of conscience, and insuring that the individual conscience is free to act without hindrance no matter what the peril might be.

  Intellectual freedom of the Calvinist spirit held by the Huguenots was freedom of the mind, believing that the mind of man had been in intellectual bondage as the result of medieval darkness, which had settled upon the world and, further, that ecclesiastical tyranny had imprisoned the minds of men and barred the way to knowledge, all of this before the Reformation.

  The Calvinist mind set recognized the belief that political freedom exemplifies the sovereignty of the people and the right of the individual to take part in the arrangements and direction of government. It inferred that this right of citizenship inheres in man by virtue of the fact that he is primarily a subject of God before he is a subject of any civil power.

  The history of the Huguenots remains a constant marvel, illustrating the power of deep faith and strong convictions. The spirit of the Huguenots emulates a great tradition. No people through the ages of history have endured more persecution, and there has been none whose spirit has been more radiant. The spirit and traditions of the Huguenots are realities demonstrated by the persecutions, perils and sufferings which they endured with unwavering faith and courage. *1*

John Calvin

Chapter One

Religious Wars and Diaspora

Our story begins in the Europe of the sixteenth century. This Europe must not be confused with the Europe of today. The modern Europe dates from the eighteenth century, with the establishment of independent political entities, based on mutually exclusive and markedly different nationalities. These nations that came into existence regarded as distinct and totally independent structures, which claimed loyalty from their inhabitants on the basis of a common national identity. The Europe of the sixteenth century was very different. National boundaries were vague - for example the border between France and Switzerland. Boundaries were supplemented by more tangible and relevant barriers of language, culture and class. A sense of national identity was generally absent. Inhabitants tended to define themselves in relation to a town or region, rather than the greater nation of which they were part. Movement across these ill-defined national frontiers was frequent and uncomplicated.

After the Hundred Years War, the church as an institution assumed an equilibrium of political power unequaled in history. This institution was to undergo profound changes in the sixteenth century and in those changes the transformation of Europe itself.

During the Middle Ages, written material had taken the form of manuscripts which had to be painstakingly copied out by hand, and were generally confined to the libraries of monasteries. By the dawn of the sixteenth century adult literacy was increasingly common, made possible primarily by the invention of the printing press.

The traditional medieval boundaries were impotent against the printed word. It was one thing to legislate against the circulation of unorthodox books; it was quite another to detect them, and present them being read. As the French authorities devised comprehensive measures to prevent the importation of seditious printed material from abroad, publishers became increasingly adept at disguising the origins of their wares. Books printed in Geneva eventually used various disguises.

As the fifteenth century gave way to the sixteenth, the need for reform and renewal of the church was everywhere evident. A number of factors, culminating in the sixteenth century, led to the growing dissatisfaction with the church - social, political and economic matters.

The rise of individual consciousness was the occasion of a new concern to relate Christianity to the needs of the individual. A generation of thinkers subsequently rose to the challenge on the eve of the Reformation. The Protestant Reformation began by Martin Luther in Germany about 1517, spread rapidly in France, especially among those having grievances against the established order of government.

Jacob Faber's translation of the New Testament, from Latin to French, first appeared in 1523. Two years later in 1525, Jacques Pavennes and Louis de Berquin, the first Huguenot martyrs, were burned at the stake. But, no persecution could stop the Reform movement as the Protestants began to take up the cause.

Religious Wars and Diaspora

Among the most famous of these thinkers was John Calvin, French Protestant theologian. Having studied theology and law, he experienced a conversion in 1533 and turned his attention to the cause of the Reformation. He began his work in Paris and was soon recognized as one of the leaders of the new movement in France. His zeal aroused the opposition of Church authorities and it became necessary for him to flee for his life. Calvin's theology diverged from Catholic doctrine in such fundamental ways as rejection of papal authority and acceptance of justification by faith alone, and the doctrine of Predestination. He also maintained that the Bible was the sole source of God's law, and that it was man's duty to interpret it, and to preserve the orderly world that God had ordained. Although Calvin never returned to France after his settlement in Geneva, he remained the leader of the French Reformation and was consulted at every step. He gave the Huguenots their creed and form of government. As Protestantism grew and developed in France it generally abandoned the Lutheran form, and took the shape of Calvinism.

The new "Reformed religion" practiced by many members of the French nobility and social middle-class, based on the belief in salvation through individual faith without the need for the intercession of a church hierarchy, and on the belief in an individual's right to interpret scriptures for themselves, placed these French Protestants in direct theological conflict with both the Catholic Church and the King of France in the theocratic system which prevailed at that time. Followers of this new Protestantism were soon accused of heresy against the Catholic government and the established religion of France, and a General Edict urging extermination of these heretics (Huguenots) was issued in 1536.

Nevertheless, Protestantism continued to spread and grow. In 1538 the first French Protestant Church was founded at Strasbourg by about 1500 refugees. The first Protestant community in France was Neaux, about the year 1546. Persecution became more rigorous. A special court was created in Paris to suppress the Huguenots, which became famous as the *Chambre Ardents* - "Chamber of Fire." About 1555 the first

Huguenot church was founded in a home in Paris based upon the teachings of John Calvin. In spite of the renewed persecution the Reformers increased in numbers. By 1560 it was estimated that twenty per cent of the population was Protestant

The number and influence of the French Huguenots continued to increase after those events, leading to an escalation in hostility and conflicts between the Catholic Church/State and the Huguenots. Finally, in 1562, some 1200 Huguenots were slain at Vassey, France, thus igniting the French Wars of Religion. The Wars of Religion between the Catholics and Huguenots would rip apart, devastate, and bankrupt France for the next three decades.

Admiral Gaspard de Coligny, principal leader of the Huguenots, aspired to establish colonies of French Protestants in the New World to relieve the situation during the early religious wars. Huguenots organized three expeditions, one to South America and two to North America. Not one of the colonies was successful.

The first one, founded under the leadership of Durand de Villegagnon at the mouth of the Rio Janeiro, in Brazil in 1555, failed. Then, Huguenot explorer Jean Ribault established Fort de la Caroline as a permanent settlement in June 1564, on St. John's River near present-day Jacksonville, Florida. It was eliminated by Spanish forces from their nearby beachhead San Augustin in September 1565. Finally, he founded ill-fated Charlesfort, a colony of Huguenots on Parris Island on the coast of South Carolina, in the early 1560s, which was abandoned.

After many armed conflicts, riots, and edicts for and against the Huguenots, the *Peace of Germain* was agreed on August 8, 1570. For the first time in over thirty years France seemed to be at peace. For two years all seemed well for the Huguenots.

Perhaps no person did more to keep alive the fires of hatred and to instigate the persecution of Huguenots as did Catherine de Medici, the Queen Regent. When Catherine's son Charles IX assumed rule, she resented the considerable influence held over him by Huguenot Admiral de Coligny. She contended that Coligny was endeavoring to draw King Charles IX into a war with Spain and resolved to have him assassinated. The attempt failed, however, and Catherine then determined to massacre *all* the Huguenot leaders.

After holding a council with the Catholic leaders, including the Duke of Anjou, Henry of Guise, the Marshal de Tavannes, the Duke of Nevers, and René de Birague, the keeper of the seals, Catherine persuaded the king that the massacre was a measure of public safety. On the evening of August 23, 1572, she succeeded in wringing authorization from him.

On St. Bartholomew's Eve, the Huguenot leaders and thousands of their followers flocked to Paris for the wedding of Henry of Bourbon and Margret of Valois. [1]

The event, known as *the Massacre of St. Bartholomew*, began early Sunday morning, August 24th. The signal of the attack - the murder of Admiral Coligny - was given by the tolling of the cathedral bells at three o'clock in the morning.

As the feast day of Saint Bartholomew dawned, all but a few of the most senior Huguenots had been killed in or around the Louvre. The elites of the French Huguenot movement, many of them experienced soldiers, were eliminated, as well as great noblemen. Neither were the humbler shown any mercy. Easily identifiable by their black-and-white clothes, few who had come to Paris, some bringing their wives and children to experience the thrill of a royal wedding, escaped. Their assailants - troops, militiamen or hate-filled Parisians - fell upon the detested men, women and children. Pregnant women were eviscerated and had their wombs cut out. Baskets filled with dead or dying small children were cast into the Seine. Most of the victims were stripped naked for any loot. Nearly all had their throats cut, and many of the men were mutilated and disemboweled. They dragged their victims through the streets of Paris. [2]

The massacre continued in Paris until September 17th. The flames of hatred fanned out over the country with orgies of killing. Once let loose, it was impossible to restrain the populace. From Paris the massacre spread to the provinces until October 3rd. François Hotman estimated the number killed in the whole of

The Huguenots of New Bordeaux

France at 50,000.

The news of the massacre was received in Rome with great joy. Catherine de Medici received the congratulations of all the Catholic powers, and Pope Gregory XIII commanded bonfires to be lighted in celebration, and a medal to be struck in honor of the great service she and the others had rendered the Church in eliminating Huguenot leaders as well as the thousands of members of the Reformed Church.

Only a handful of senior Huguenots escaped, yet each carried with them the spores to start a fresh civil war. The survivors resolved upon a desperate resistance. Huguenots established a political party in 1575, and resorted to armed resistance.

A temporary peace came with the Huguenot King Henry of Navarre's victory at the battle of Ivry in 1590. Ruler of a bankrupt, exhausted France, King Henry IV determined to end its religious struggles. His committee of scholars and diplomats drew up the *Edict of Nantes,* promulgated April 13, 1598, a religious bill of rights for all French people, both Catholic and Huguenot. The Edict of Nantes, signed by Henry IV, ended the Wars of Religion, and allowed the Huguenots some religious freedoms, including free exercise of their religion in twenty specified towns of France.

After Henry's assassination in 1610, the Huguenots' rights steadily diminished. The Edict of Nantes remained the law of the land, but the freedoms and privileges granted the Huguenots were by decree extricated. LaRochelle, the stronghold of the Huguenots, capitulated on October 28, 1628, after a siege of more than a year, in which two-thirds of its inhabitants perished.

After warring against the Huguenots from 1621 to 1629, the French government tried to force them into the Catholic fold through a series of repressive measures. This harassment was intensified under King Louis XIV.

As part of the clamp-down, Huguenot civil rights were progressively removed. Between 1657 and 1685, about 300 rulings, often suggested by the Catholic clergy, were made against the Huguenots. The rulings attacked every aspect of their lives. They were stripped of all civil rights. Ultimately a vast

Religious Wars and Diaspora

array of professions, such as medicine, law, and even midwifery, were forbidden. Huguenots were disbarred from holding public office. Protestant marriages were declared null and void. Armed soldiers called "dragoons" billeted in houses of Huguenots with a view to intimidating the occupants. The privacy of the home was broken up, valuables were taken, defenseless women were ravished, and all manners of horror were perpetrated by the brutal soldiery. Any remonstration against authorities was met by the most horrible punishment, even death. The dragoons were authorized to brutalize families, make them suffer loss of sleep, and destroy possessions, the purpose being to force Huguenots to convert to Catholicism.

In 1663, conversion from Catholicism to Huguenot became illegal. Restriction were put into place as to where the Huguenots could live. Another measure made it possible for Huguenot children at the age of seven to become Catholics against their parents' wishes. Huguenot parents were obliged to finance the education their children received from Jesuits or other Catholic instructors.

Another method of suppressing the Huguenots was the secretive *Compagnie du Saint-Sacrement*, an organization with a vast network of spies covering the whole of France that used tactics from pressure to obstruction, manipulation to denunciation with every means to weaken the Huguenot community, even within family households. And still the Huguenots persevered and remained in France.

Finally King Louis XIV realized that his "persuasion and legislation" for exterminating the Huguenot movement were not succeeding. In his final attempt to extirpate Protestantism from his lands, he signed the *Edict of Fontainebleau* in 1685, revoking the Edict of Nantes, perhaps the most famous event in Louis XIV's long reign (1643-1715), and undoubtedly the most flagrant political and religious blunder in the history of France.

Although the desire to eliminate Protestants and Protestant power was long standing, the Revocation itself was the child of the late 1670s persecution, not its parent - an achievement Louis XIV had long desired but never dared hope was attainable until its very eve. The Revocation was, then, new as well as familiar - a single event occurring in October 1685

whose origins easily extended back into the previous decade.
The already-diminished plight of the Huguenots worsened. Massive persecutions came again. Unfaltering Huguenots chose to worship secretly. With their meeting places destroyed and their public worship banned, they turned to the "Church of the Desert," or underground worship. This, despite the fact that people who held such meetings risked being sentenced to death, according to a law passed in July 1686.

The Huguenot exodus began. This emigration has been called a *veritable diaspora*. Many of France's most skilled craftsmen, farmers, merchants, and her most brilliant scholars fled. These refugees initially settled in the nearest Protestant sanctuaries available to them - Geneva, the Netherlands, and England. But as prospects dimmed for returning to France, many sought new homes for a permanent exile. These second migrations took Huguenot refugees far from their native France and Europe to places as remote as the Germanies, South Africa, and America. Over 7,000 reached the shores of America, with large concentrations in New England, New York, Pennsylvania, Virginia, and South Carolina.

At least 200,000 men, women, and children migrated. This would have been a massive exodus even in modern times. In fact, it was the largest population movement in early modern Europe aside from the expulsion of the Moors from Spain, and it was all the more remarkable in the fact of crude transportation and social milieu that limited population mobility for most people to relatively constricted regional movements.

The extraordinary demographic breadth of the exodus reveals the deep effect of government terrorism in Protestant France. Where young, single men had dominated voluntary migration even in the early modern era, the Huguenot diaspora sent large numbers of women, and often old women, out of France. Women headed as many as half of the refugee households in late seventeenth-century London. Moreover, half of these women were over fifty-five years of age and some had reached their seventies. Children also comprised an unusually large proportion of the fleeing population.

Survival through conversion turned out to be a choice of some Huguenots in France following the Revocation in 1685.

Religious Wars and Diaspora

Although France had suddenly become totally Catholic, close to 600,000 Huguenots still lived within its boundaries. The Revocation put an end to the official existence of France's most important religious minority but failed to eradicate Calvinism. The three-generation conversion pattern existed - the first *clung to the Huguenot faith*, the second practiced a *Catholicism de façade*, while the third was *truly Catholic*. Although seriously undermined, French Protestantism survived as the church went underground, and, a significant number devised ways to maintain their faith. As a matter of fact, in 1726, a seminary was opened in Lausanne, Switzerland. By the first quarter of the eighteenth century, the Huguenot church was born again, and in 1760, France had a Calvinist population of about a half million.

As the eighteenth century drew to a close public opinion began to revolt against the persecution of the Huguenots. The *Promulgation of the Edict of Toleration* in November 1787 partially restored the civil and religions rights of Huguenots in France. In 1789 the *Declaration of the Rights of Man* affirmed the liberty of religion and the legal standing of the Reformed Church was recognized. Influenced by the United States Declaration of Independence and *the Enlightenment*, it asserted the equality of all men, the sovereignty of the people, and the inalienable rights of the individual to liberty, property, and security

There are about 900,000 Protestants in France today, or no more than two per cent of the population. However, they make up in energy what their group lacks in size, and their importance to their country is enormous. The liberal professions and the civil service are packed with Protestants. They make up more than one fifth of the faculties of the universities. High finance, to no small extent, is a Protestant domain. Most of the country's leading private banks are owned by a handful of Protestant clans. [3]

The Reverend Jean Louis Gibert

Chapter Two

The Pastor of the Desert

In the Cévennes region, noted for its religious fervor, militant Huguenots called Camisards revolted in 1702. Responding to the Camisards' ambushes and night-time attacks, government troops burned villages. Although sporadic Huguenot attacks continued for some time, by 1710 the might of King Louis' army had crushed the Camisards.

The Reverend Jean Louis Gibert, fearless Huguenot "pastor of the desert," and leader of the seventh and last settlement of Huguenots in South Carolina, was born June 29, 1722, in the stony, vine-clad hills of Lunes, Languedoc, Southern France. He was the eldest of three sons of Louise Guy and Pierre Gibert I. His second brother was Pierre Gibert II, and his youngest, Etienne. The family was Protestant. How long the Gibert family had adhered to the reformed faith of Calvin is not known; most probably for more than a hundred years. Calvinism flourished at an early date in Languedoc and by 1560 the majority of the population was Protestant.

The Huguenots of New Bordeaux

Prior to the birth of Jean Louis Gibert, the fierce Camisard War (1702-1711) in the Cévennes, between the State and Catholics on one side and the Huguenots on the other, had come to an end. But the stories about de Baville, the cruel prosecutor of Protestants in Languedoc, and the brave Camisard leaders, Roland and Cavalier, surely stirred the imagination and kindled fires within many young and impressionable minds. To this were added stories of a new leader, Antoine Court, who from about 1710 to 1730, by his peaching and organizing efforts had begun to "restore" Protestantism in that part of France.

Jean Louis Gibert was endowed with a lively intellect, a forceful character, and lots of energy. His piety was nurtured by his reading of the Bible, his family environment and his attendance at the prescribed assemblies. As early as allowed, he began to accompany a "Pastor of the Desert" (wilderness) as a young student under the pastor's tutelage (probably Jean Combes). At the age of twenty-three, he was already an understudy and assisted as a secretary to the Synod in Cévennes, August 18, 1745. In 1746 the Synod authorized the enrollment of Gibert in the Lausanne Theological Seminary, Switzerland. There he studied for three years, October 1746 to September 1749. He was one of a distinguished group of graduates who were to make reputations for themselves.

He began his work as a "Pastor of the Desert" in the Hautes, Cévennes in 1750 but stayed there only a year. He requested that he be allowed to serve the churches in two of the western provinces, Saintonge and Poitou, where there were very few pastors to serve the many scattered Protestant families. Here in the western provinces he was to do great work over a period of twelve years and to accomplish there what Antoine Court and Pierre Corrteiz had done for the churches in Languedoc. In time he was to be known as the "Apostle of Saintonge."

In 1751 he traveled to Saintonge. For the better part of his pastoral life in France he worked diligently in the western provinces. Much had to be done if Protestantism in this part of

The Pastor of the Desert

France was to be restored. He dared much for the Cause. His code name was "Cévennes." He was ever on the go and a man of action. In the numerous woods and forests, on the banks of rivers, in remote sand dunes along the seashore, he summoned the faithful to worship. His wearing apparel while preaching was a square black cap, a long straight coat and a blue silk collar. He chose places where his followers could be protected from the King's soldiers. Runners were stationed near garrisons to watch the movements of the mounted dragoons (troops). Sites were chosen with ready exits. Watchmen were placed on hills and crags and with torches for signals. If the assembly was attacked by troops, the pastor was the leader. God had admirably qualified Jean Louis Gibert for his work. He was of middle stature, black hair and grey eyes, with a strong cast of countenance. He enjoyed robust health and had the courage to meet any emergency. He was cool in the face of danger, made quick, and sound decisions, and inspired others to follow. Above all, he was a man ever on the go.

During 1755, with some relaxation of persecution in Saintonge, he began in a small way to execute a plan long dear to him and one in which he could take the initiative, the building of wooden houses fo prayer and worship. Sometimes a barn was renovated or some other structure, for this purpose. The execution of this plan became a part of his work for some five years. Some of the structures, of course, were burned or torn down by the dragoons, but others were left disturbed.

In 1756, Pastor Gibert attended the National Synod in the Hautes, Cévennes and seized this opportunity to visit his family and friends in and around Lunes. His mother, Louise Guy Gibert was still living but his father had died before 1751.

The Reverend Jean Louis Gibert had many narrow escapes. Finally, *in absentia, he was condemned by judgements on July 14, 1756, to be put to death by hanging, and his body to remain for twenty-four hours on the forked gibbet.* The Bishop of Saintes was most anxious to execute Pastor Gibert in order to curb the growth of Protestantism in his bishopric. Fortunately, the authorities were never able to apprehend him.

Sometime in 1756 or 1757, Pierre Dugas became a pastor in Saintonge. He and Pastor Gibert became great friends and at some point they edited together a collection of prayers. This may well have been his only literary work.

Unfortunately in 1758, once more, the Protestants in all the provinces began to feel great pressure, and renewed persecutions because of the Ordinance of November 1, 1757, proclaimed by Louis XV.

Pastor Gibert's work in building small houses of worship was only partially successful, but he managed to extend this work into several provinces other than Saintonge.

Sometime, about 1760, his mind began to turn toward a larger plan, the colonization of persecuted Protestants. His plan was to go to England and enlist the aid of Archbishop of Canterbury Stecker. Fortunately, in 1761, three new pastors began their pastorates in Saintonge: Pierre Boutiton, Gibert's future brother-in-law was one of the three.

On April 6, 1761, Pastor Gibert arrived in London and met with Revs. Majendie and Muyssen, pastors at the French church of Savoye. Majendie was to become most helpful. Gibert had prepared a well-worded letter to be sent to Stecker, the Archbishop, on behalf of churches and pastors in four provinces: Saintonge, Angoumois, Perigord, and Bordelais. He knew that Stecker was very much concerned about the persecutions of Protestants in France. Gibert's forthright letter covers four printed pages in the biography *Les Freres Gibert*. His main objective was to have Secker obtain from King George III grants of land in North America for Protestant refugees from France, and financial aid to transport them and support them for a year until they could get settled. Majendie, most probably, delivered the letter to the Archbishop in person and added his support. Stecker, in turn, passed the letter on to Lord Hardwicke, the Duke of Newcastle, Mr. Pitt, Lord Bute and the secretaries of four ministries. All four ministries agreed in general. And within a short time the Archbishop had a conversation with King George III on the matter. King George III was favorable. Pastor Gibert was to assure that the colonists would conform to the Anglican worship, have bishops, establish silk culture in the colony and manufacture coarse or linen cloth.

On April 23, 1761, Gibert had a heartening conference with the Archbishop, then made his way secretly back to France.

In 1762 Pastor Gibert was again in England. He was ready to risk anything now to achieve his bold plan. He was especially troubled that, with the Seven Year War between England and France coming to a close (the Treaty of Paris was signed in 1763), the French government might resort to harsher persecutions upon the Protestants if for no other reason than to give the returning solders something to do. Gibert believed that, on the whole, the Huguenot pastors in England would support the colonization plan, but he wished to make certain of their support. Pastor Pierre Boudet, of a Bristol church, (better known in France as "Gautier") who had worked long in Normandy and had been a schoolmate with Jean Louis Gibert at the Lausanne Seminary, wrote a letter to Majendie (dated December 21, 1762), urging that the project should be placed on a policy level. His view was that M. de Goutrespac at Lousanne, under the name of Court de Gebelin, who then was the agent general for correspondence with the Protestant churches in France, should send a letter to all the church leaders to seek their views and assistance. This letter to Majendie was communicated to Archbishop Stecker who sent it to Lord Egremont (Pitt's successor), who placed it before King George III. The King approved and suggested that the assurances, which he made to Gibert in April 1761, become a part of a letter to the French Protestant leaders in France as proposed by Pastor Gautier.

In March 1763, Pastor Gibert went again to England. Time was running short. The remaining months were busy and difficult ones for him. Huguenots in France, who knew of his

The Huguenots of New Bordeaux

colonization plan and wanted to join the group, had to have a sufficient lead time for arrival in England before the boat sailed, despite mishaps and unavoidable delays. The usual routes of escape were via Holland, Switzerland and the French maritime ports. Few in France could have known of the exact sailing date from England.

Pastor Gibert petitioned the British Lords of Trade for not less than 20,000 acres of land on which to establish the Huguenot colony and village in a lengthy letter read at the Court of St. James in London on July 29, 1763. Following is an excerpt from his letter in which he requested its location either along the Ohio River or on the Savannah River in South Carolina :

"... Que comme M. Jenkinson a fait entendre au dit Gibert qu'il étoit inutile qu'il demanda d'autres terres que dans la Caroline il est très disposé à s'en contenter, mais il ne peut s'empêcher d'observer en même tems que le climat étant si chaud le Gouvernement ne retirera pas d'aussi grands ni d'aussi prompts avantages de la culture des vignes et des Muiers qu'on auroit pu s'en promettre dans un climat un peu plus froid tel que le sont les Rives de l'Ohio sur lesquelles il avoit d'abord porté ses vues, Qu'enfin puisque la chose convient sans doute mieux sur ce pied aux vues du Ministre, il prend donc la liberté de demander, qu'on lui assigne, qu'on mesure, et qu'on donne les ordres les plus efficaces, pour que sa Colonie soit mise en possession, dès le moment de son arrivée; de trente milles en quarré de terrain, sur la Rive Orientale de la Rivière Savannah, â choisir entre la ville de Purisburg et le Fort Moore.

"Pour que de ces trente milles en quarré il en soit mesuré trente mille acres pour le Township de la Ville qu'ils se proposent de bâtir sans aucun rétard ou delai."

Great Britain's motive in sending the Huguenots to South Carolina was a mixture of Christian benevolence and economic shrewdness. The Crown wished to attract foreign Protestants who were allegedly experts in the production of wine, silk, and olive oil. Their objective was to rapidly settle their North American colonies at the lowest possible cost while introducing new commodities that would develop a lucrative trade. At the same time, overwhelmed with Huguenot refugees and unwilling to populate its North American dependencies at the expense of its demographic growth, England encouraged such a policy in helping Huguenot refugees to meet the cost of the transatlantic voyage while ridding herself of them.

The Gibert Family Home, near le Lunès, France.

Chapter Three

The Long Voyage

British King George III agreed to settle the Huguenots in North America. Pastor Gibert initiated the first phase of the bold scheme to actually move his flock out of France and establish a colony in South Carolina. Pastor Gibert, condemned to death by the French government seven years earlier for his Calvinist preaching, directed operations from his London base. He maintained communication with the several scattered groups that would travel secretly on a moment's notice. The plan was to rendevous at Royan, a small seaport town and Huguenot bastion of less than a thousand inhabitants located on the west bank of the Gironde at its mouth, sixty-three miles below and north northwest of Bordeaux in west France. Timing was of essence in order to avoid arousing the suspicion of authorities. During the Wars of Religion, Royan had been a center of Calvinism, and in 1622 sustained an eight-day siege by the troops of Louis XIII.

The Long Voyage

The plan worked. The refugees, traveling by land and water from their various homes in the south of France, reached Royan safely where a barque awaited them. A barque was a small sailing ship with three to five masts, all of them square-rigged except the after mast, which was fore-and-aft rigged.

A precise departure time was crucial. Detection by the French authorities would foil the plan and jeopardize the lives of the refugees. Also, the Royan harbor at a high tide was accessible only to vessels drawing from eight to ten feet, and at low water was dry.

The refugees boarded the barque. The aging sailing vessel, manned by a short-handed crew of seamen, slid quietly out of the harbor, and headed northward toward the English Channel and Plymouth, England, on August 9, 1763. [1]

As the ship spread its sails to the breeze on the first link of what would be a long and grueling voyage, the Huguenots crowded the deck to gaze upon the receding shore. The bright morning sun gilded the coast with all the rich and varied colors of a summer landscape. A charming softness, a peculiar beauty, hung around the lovely vales and verdant slopes. The refugees, no doubt, felt a tantalizing power, like never before, as they feasted their eyes for the last time on their native France. Behind the vine-clad hills, now robed in solemn grandeur, they reminisced of things from the past, beloved friends left behind and the soil that gave them birth; all the associations of early life, the fond remembrance of childhood's home, their native hills and woods and streams, their school days, the joys of manhood, mingled with the terrible persecutions from which they had so recently escaped, crowded their minds, and filled their hearts and eyes to overflowing. The shore faded until there was nothing to see but the wide expanse of water - their whole destiny riding on a frail ship and their moving faith in God. [2]

Pierre Moragné, one of the Huguenot refugees aboard ship, recorded an account of the harrowing journey. He came from the Dordogne Valley near St. Foy in the parish of St. Avid du Tizac. From the sale of his estate in France, he had obtained £300 with which he was able to advance the colony, most of them rather poor, the sum of £31, 16s, for provisioning the ship. His first wife died while the Huguenots were in England. Excerpts from Moragné's journal are shown in "*italic.*"

From Royan, for six days the barque carrying the refugees edged the coast of France, crossed the English Channel, and docked at Dartmouth, England, to take on supplies.

Moragné wrote, "*August 16th We have put into the Port of D'Artimone, ten leagues from Plymouth, where we have taken in some refreshments, after having been without taste of anything for some time during the voyage.*"

The refugees moved out of the Dartmouth harbor on August 22nd. The next day they encountered a horrific storm while still in the English Channel. This new experience terrified the passengers.

"*August 23rd In a contrary wind an opening was made for the water in a private part of our Barque, which soon alarmed us all even to the Captain, who had not bethought himself to set sail for landing at the first Port; and, we, of our side, worked incessantly with buckets and with the pump to keep the water out of the Captain's cabin. We stood in the water four hours; but by the grace of God, we reached land, with great danger of ship-wreck, by a very narrow passage between two rocks:- We could not pass elsewhere; and after having put in order my affairs, one named Bonique Siragieus, some others and myself, preferring to make the journey by land, parted, on the same day, from the Barque, afterwards to be repaired in fair weather.*"

Two days later, the barque carrying the Huguenot refugees dropped anchor in the harbor at Plymouth. There they were lodged in buildings, which formerly had housed prisoners. They would remain quartered there in England anxiously awaiting departure for South Carolina for four long months. [3]

The refugees mustered for enumeration at Plymouth on

The Long Voyage

November 22, 1763. *Note variable spelling of names recorded on this roster and subsequent rosters. Given names are often English versions of the French.*

Liste des Protestants Refugie's actuellement a' Plymouth pour se rendre en Amerique dans les possessions de sa majest' George troisieme Roy de la Grande Bretagne sous la conduite & direction de Jean Louis Gibert, Pasteur:

Name of Male	Age	Occupation
1. Jacques Touzeau	30	Catechiste
2. Daniel Due	31	Capitaine de Navire
3. Pre Pierre Don	25	Dr. En Medicine ou Chisurgia
4. Barthelemy Bouigue	22	Chirurgien
5. Jacques Boutiton	51	Laboureur
6. Pierre Boutiton	20	Laboureur
7. Jean Roger	45	Commercant
8. Pierre Roger	21	Laboureur
9. Jean Roger	20	Laboureur
10. Matthieu Bereau	35	Laboureur
11. Jean Bereau	32	Tonelieur
12. Matthieu Bereau	23	Tonelieur
13. Jacob Chardavoine	17	Marin
14. Pierre Moragne	22	Laboureur
15. Paul Nino	19	Perruquier
16. Louis Villaret	26	Boulanger & cultivr. de Muriers
17. Jean Gout	19	Perruquier
18. Pierre Lioron	27	Jardinier & cultr. de Muriers
19. Jean Frisille	48	Pillote
20. Pierre Gollin	31	Marin
21. Pierre Gollin	7	
22. Andre Audouin	24	Marin

23. Jacob Baylard	23	Masson	
24. Jacob Langel	45	Charon	
25. Jean Faveraud	24	Laboureur	
26. Jacques Labrousse	35	Labr.	
27. Etienne Labrousse	7		
28. Francois Gross	26	Labr.	
29. Etienne Favereau	30	Labr.	
30. Pierre Rolland	30	Menuisier	
31. Pierre Roquemore	22	Bonnetier	
32. Jean Bonneau	28	Labr.	
33. Jean Boutin	24	Menuisier	
34. Jean Vidau	23	Labr.	
35. Louis Vidau	22	Vigneron	
36. Pierre Dumas	30	Tonnelier	
37. Pierre Renond	36	Menuisier	
38. Jacques Gereau	34	Menuisier	
39. Joseph Rolland	27	Tailleur	
40. Jean Audibert	22	Vigneron	
41. Pierre Chuseau	34	Tisseran	
42. Pierre Lartigue	18	Masson	
43. Jean Boyer	20	Vigneron	
44. Jean Priolot	24	Vigneron	
45. Jean Brieau	24	Charon	
46. Pre Roquemore	18	Fabrig en Bas	
47. Francois Bayle	24	Tailleur	
48. Jean Bouchillon	19	Labr.	
49. Andre Guillebeau	25	Charpr.	
50. Francois Prouillac	18	Vigneron	
51. Jean Roquemore	36	Taneur	
52. Jacques Langel	40	Vigneron	
53. Denis Langel	3		
54. Jacques Langel	2		
55. Jean Dupuis	12	Cordonnier	
56. Pierre Bayle	19	Vigneron	
57. Joseph Bouchillon	22	Vigneron	

The Long Voyage

58. Jean Antony	20	Sciller
59. Pierre Sundre	20	Tonneller
60. Jean la Faye	27	
61. Jacques la Faye	7	
62. Jean la Faye	5	
63. Jean la Faye	3	
64. Antoine Farastau	34	Vigon
65. Antoine Gabeau	7	
66. Colas Bordajeau	33	Labr.
67. Pierre Bordajeau	6	
68. Jean Bordajeau	8	
69. Mathieu Festal	35	Preceptr.
70. Charles Bouchonaud	19	Pilotn.
71. Nic. Bouchonaud	15	Marin
72. Jean Bellefaye	56	March.
73. Jean Dom	16	Marin
74. Pierre Reigne	36	Marin
75. Jean Castan	18	Vigneron
76. Pierre Chareau	24	Charpr.
77. Jean Bellotte	50	Fabr. D-etoffe
78. Pierre Elie Bellotte	19	Marin
79. Jean Arnaud Bellotte	3	
80. Theodore Guay	23	Jaedr. & Potier
81. Andre Wagnon	37	
82. Abram Jacob	37	Cordonr.
83. Daniel Jacob	3	
84. Jean Bte. Gautier	45	Tailleur
85. Theodore Gautier	7	
86. Samuel Bollomay	23	Cordr.
87. Jn. Bte. Delonay	45	Tisserand
88. Jn. Bte. Delonay	10	
89. Antonio Delonay	4	
90. Jacques Delonay	1	
91. Jn. Bte. Petit	27	Tailleur
92. Antoine Billaud	36	Vigneron

93. Nichs. Basson	23	Vigneron
94. Pierre Barbier	23	Marin
95. Etienne Thomas	12	Vigneron
96. N. Labrousse	1	
97. Pierre Langel	11	
98. Antne. Herport	26	Notaiare
99. Francois Branton	23	Labr.
100. Jean Pierre Beillard	33	Boulr.
101. Pierre Boyer	20	Boutonnier
102. Jean Eymery	32	Reliur
103. Pre. Garrineau	26	Masson
104. Jn. Pre. Nicholas	27	Marin
105. Pierre Boutiton	50	Pasteur
106. Louis Villaret	45	Pr. Les Murrs. & c
107. Ant. Jos. Labbe	34	Precepteur
108. Jn. Louis Husson	25	Charpr.
109. Pre. Nicholas Piron	26	Perruqr.
110. Francis Gerard	35	Tailleur
111. Jn. Fs. Poitevin	35	
112. Jn. Fs. Poitevin	2	

Name of Female	Age
1. Marguerite Tessandier	54
2. Jean Boutiton	21
3. Marthe Armagnieu	30
4. Jeanne Roudier	20
5. Anne Latour	25
6. Suzanne Latour	20
7. Anne Coureau	50
8. Marie Bouchonau	14
9. Anne Lespine	42
10. Marte. Roger	22
11. Eliz. Gregoire	33
12. Anne Beraud	7
13. Marie Beraud	4

14. Anne Beraud	38
15. Eliz. Bien Aime	4
16. Jeanne Blanchet	32
17. Marie Labrousse	3
18. Marie Roujon	40
19. Judith Fresille	10
20. Marie Fresille	8
21. Susanne Fresille	4
22. Jeanne Lievre	36
23. Jeanne Gollin	1
24. Jeanne Caris	30
25. Francoise Renateau	23
26. Anne Bellefaye	11
27. Jeanne Bonneaud	36
28. Ledie Gognet	46
29. Marie Madelaine Bellote	16
30. Me. Judith Bellote	8
31. Susanne Alexandre	27
32. N. Gautier	1
33. Marie Favereau	30
34. Marie Quate	25
35. Susanne Lafonde	55
36. Jeanne Seguin	30
37. Marie Roquemore	4
38. Jeanne Alegresse	33
39. Anne Langel	5
40. Marie Seiral	54
41. Cecile Bayle	22
42. Marie Maginier	25
43. Marie Verdiere	35
44. Marie Ferasteau	25
45. Marie Ferasteau	1
46. Francoise Sacboville	32
47. Marie Bordajeau	10
48. Jeanne Bordajeau	1

49. Marie Vilke   16
50. Susanne Isabeau Joly   37
51. Marie Judith Jacob   5
52. Francoise Favereau   26
53. Marie de la Mare   33
54. Marie Delaunnay   12
55. Marie Reparon   22
56. Marie Thomas   31
57. Anne Julne. Morin   35
58. Ane. Julne. Poitevin   7
59. Jeanne le Fevre   24
60. Marie Husson   1
61. Amel Guilliame   -

(A total of 112 males and 61 females) 4

During their stay in Plymouth, England, there was a move among the Huguenots to seek settlement on St. John's River in East Florida rather than in South Carolina. Records do not indicate the reason, but a good guess would be that upon reaching Plymouth the refugees learned the settlements in the South Carolina back country had just recently experienced the horrific Cherokee War (1760-61) with many casualties, and that there yet remained a very real threat of further attacks from the Cherokee as well as the Creek Indians.

Pastor Pierre Boutiton, on behalf of the refugees, communicated their desire for establishing the Huguenot colony in East Florida to Lord Halifax who passed the request to the Earl of Hillsborough and the Lords Commissioners for Trade and Plantations. It is interesting here that *Pastor Boutiton*, rather than *Pastor Gibert*, presented the request to the Commissioners. Up to this point, Pastor Gibert had executed all negotiations with British authorities.

The Commissioners in session on Thursday, October 20, 1763 instructed Pastor Boutiton to, "reduce his prepositions in writing," and requested him to, "attend the Board to-morrow morning at 11 o'clock." Pastor Boutiton met with the Board on October 21st and, "presented a memorial containing several propositions in respect to the establishment of these people in East-Florida, and the lands to be granted, and other allowances to be made to them," The Board abstained from reporting "any opinion to His Majesty until they shall receive the sentiments of the Lords Commissioners of the Treasury." On November 1st Hillsborough presented a letter from the Secretary of the Treasury; ordering, "the said letter do lye by for further consideration." The request for change in settlement location never got so far as His Majesty. After several meetings, Hillsborough directed officials on November 8th to pursue the earlier plan agreed upon by the Commissioners and Pastor Jean Louis Gibert for sending the Huguenots to South Carolina.

To be precise, the South Carolina location on which the Huguenots finally settled was not in accordance with the agreement between Pastor Gibert and the Crown. The agreement stipulated that a township for the refugees would be located on the Savannah River between Purrysburgh and Fort Moore. Purrysburgh was a Swiss Huguenot settlement in South Carolina just a few miles up river from Savannah, Georgia. Fort Moore, was located at Beach Island across the river from Augusta, Georgia.

But, King George III had his own agenda. He was interested in bringing about quick settling of the South Carolina back country following the Cherokee War. His Commissioners designated a location further north in the thinly settled back country, the strategy being to create a buffer against further Indian uprisings.

J. Pownall, for the Lords Commissioners issued orders on November 18, 1763, directing Charles Jenkinson, Secretary to Lords of Treasury for "passage of the French Protestants to Charles-Town, South-Carolina." An enclosure stipulated, "Terms to be inserted in Mr. McNutt's contract to carry two hundred French Protestants to South-Carolina. That the said

McNutt will furnish a proper vessel, staunch and well equipt in all respects for their voyage. That the people shall be accommodated with berths and provisions as customary in all passenger ships from this country and Ireland, that is to say:

Berths, of 6 feet by 18 inches each)
6 lb. of bread; 6 lb. of beef   ) per week to each person
1 lb. of butter   )

2 quarts of water per day to each person. When cheese or flour is required a deduction is to be made for it of some other article. The full use of fire all day, and their provisions good in quality. ₅

Pastor Gibert and his refugees vacated their quarters in Plymouth on Christmas Day 1763, and commenced going aboard a British brigantine, the *Friendship*, commanded by Captain George Perkins. A brigantine in that era was a two-masted sailing ship, square-rigged on the foremast and having a fore-and-aft mainsail with square main topsails. They expected to reach South Carolina by the end of February.

"25th December. We have commenced going aboard of a vessel, destined to bear us from Plymouth to America, at Charles Town, in South Carolina. Our sojourn at Plymouth has been much longer than we anticipated, and we have undergone much trouble, which is too bitter to speak of here."

But, for a full month the wind and current remained calm. The *Friendship's* sails flapped listlessly without even a ghost of a breeze as the ship simply lay in the bay at Plymouth. Of course, there were no weather forecasts available to captains of sailing ships in that day.

Finally, the wind, having been so long in dead calm, raised enough to fill the sails of the *Friendship* and gently carry her out to sea - this on the 25th of January, 1764.

"Faithful to setting out with the first good wind, the want of which has withheld us till now, we departed with a little breeze, favorable enough for carrying us out of the channel."

Only two days at sea, a fierce gale set in. The unrelenting winds buffeted the *Friendship* unmercifully. Great

The Long Voyage

waves swelled and crashed down to batter the ship's stern with tons of white water. The brigantine ran baremasted, except for the jib and spritsail that hopefully held her on a westerly course, so that only her stern took the smashing impact of the waves. The vessel pitched and tossed and rose sickeningly to the dreadful discomfort of her cargo of terrified refugee passengers, her bowsprit angling skyward, hanging there for long minutes repeatedly before a caprice of wind and water dropped her downward again.

The fury of the gale lasted three days before blowing itself out. By the time the gale broke, the shipload of Huguenots had been driven totally off the course, so much so that now the *Friendship* had swung around and sailed back in the direction from which she had left. When experience-hardened Captain Perkins was able to, he nosed the vessel into a quiet haven in a roadstead at Farbret on the English Channel, some eleven leagues east of (and on the farther side of Plymouth) on the coast of England, and dropped anchor.

"January 27th, 28th, 29th. We have had a great tempest, and great risk of perishing, as, not being yet out of the channel, we were stranded on some rocks; and we have had many of our clothes and much of our bedding wet, from the waves of the sea, rising on the deck of the vessel: on which account we have been obliged to lay to, in the road-stead of Farbret, which is eleven leagues further than Plymouth from Charles Town."

Moragné's journal now portrayed a frustrated group of travel-weary Huguenots. Morale obviously reached a low point after the months of delays and sailing on stormy seas that surely must have tested their faith. At this point, the refugees were yet no nearer to their new home in America than when they left Royan, France, five months ago. Some passengers were likely ill from the harsh elements, scurvy, and seasickness. Most of the refugees had become quarrelsome and ill-tempered – these 173 passengers tightly packed on a brigantine. Some of the passengers complained loudly to the captain about the food.

"*A rebellion took place by most of the passengers against the Captain on report of the meats, which were not found good; and many hard words were spoken, which brought down the wrath of God upon us; and the next day we set sail.*"

The *Friendship* slid out of the roadstead at Farbret on February 14th, then stopped on the 17th at Plymouth for a stay of five days to give the passengers a break, and to get the matter of the food complaints settled. Inspectors in Plymouth claimed they found no problem with the food.

Once again the ship bearing the sojourning Huguenots made sail on the 22nd of February 1764, heading across the passage between Plymouth, England and Charles Town, South Carolina. This time was different.

The water was calm, usually with only a little swell, and the wind that blew in was mostly gentle. The captain took full advantage as the broad sails of the *Friendship* bended to the wind and now made good speed. Incredibly, the rest of the voyage went on with uncommon smoothness - compared to what they had already experienced - except a mishap that occurred a couple of days before the end of the voyage.

A spirit-lifting event for the passengers occurred on March 17th when the *Friendship* rendezvoused with a vessel returning to England from South Carolina.

Passengers got a scare that passed quickly on April 2nd with the sighting of a "whirlwind."

"*We have had some showers and dark clouds as a whirlwind came over the waters of the sea: - It was very dangerous, if unhappily it had our vessel; and the Captain had delayed reefing sail to avoid the danger of the water; one moment after we heard a clap of thunder, which soon made us shut the hatches in apprehension of a great tempest.*"

Passengers now began to see seaweed swirling in the water, indicating they were nearing land. On April 10th there was great rejoicing as they began to catch a glimpse of the palmetto-clad South Carolina coast line.

But, celebration was of short duration. The *Friendship* bottomed out on a sand bar just offshore from Charles Town. The impact against the sea floor greatly alarmed the passengers who feared the ship's masts would surely collapse. The collision left the ship helplessly stuck. The captain ordered the refugees to discard personal cargo to cause the vessel to draw less water. They complied and the vessel raised.

The *Friendship,* conveying the Huguenot refugees, crossed the bar in the harbor of Charles Town, South Carolina, and dropped anchor on the 12th of April 1764.

"We commenced seeing the shores of America, which greatly rejoiced us, having been forty-seven days complete without the sight of aught but the heavens and the waters;- but that joy was soon changed to sadness: for we found ourselves run aground on a bank of sand, on which our vessel struck so hard, that we expected her masting would come to pieces by the shock, which would certainly have happened if the wind had been high.

We all commenced immediately to lighten the vessel by throwing into the sea everything of least value; and managed thereby to extricate ourselves from great danger."

When Pastor Gibert's flock of Huguenots came ashore, Charles Town residents offered a warm welcome. State authorities provided temporarily lodging in barracks. The French Church donated food to the refugees to tide them over until they could be settled into housing to await the trek to their final destination in the back country. [6]

Charles Town, a booming, boisterous town and the state capital, ranked fourth in population behind Philadelphia, New York, and Boston. Great Britain had just emerged from the Seven Years' War as the dominant power of Western Europe and North America. France relinquished Canada and the Mississippi Valley, and Britain acquired Florida from Spain. The leading merchants in Charles Town, however, had accumulated vast wealth during the war and were now passionately interested in spending it. They built handsome houses, imported expensive silks and satins to wear, went to the theater and to concerts and balls, bought luxurious carriages, and dressed their slaves in grand and costly liveries. The name of the city would be changed from Charles Town to Charleston in 1783.

The population of Charles Town included Huguenots in 1764. Migration had occurred during the period of the Revocation as a result of the religious wars. By 1686 Huguenot immigrants had begun building their "French Church" on upper Church Street.

More than a half century earlier in 1703, a visitor to Charles Town observed, "mixing together in the town's streets were hucksters hawking their wares, indentured white servants, sailors, farmers or 'planters,' fur traders, and African slaves. It was a potpourri of nationalities and racial groups and a corresponding Babel of languages and sounds."

Also, the French and Indian War had fueled the economy of Charles Town and concentrated even greater wealth and power in the hands of a tiny elite at the top of society, but life deteriorated for many of those at the bottom. Wealthy merchants bought at bargain rates French vessels taken as prizes by the British Navy. Cooper River in the city appeared so choked with vessels that it resembled a "floating market," carrying commodities to distant ports under the protection of British war ships. [7]

Charles Town had suffered the worst smallpox epidemic in its history beginning in January 1760. During the height of the epidemic, hundreds of townspeople died. Believing that God was punishing a sinful people through a visitation of smallpox, acting Governor William Bull declared a "Day of Fasting ... and Prayer." The smallpox epidemic ended shortly in late June. About 9 percent of the town's population had succumbed to the disease. [8]

The Long Voyage

Pastor Gibert's Huguenots refugees were called into Council chambers on April 18, 1764. They took the oath of allegiance, and prayed for bounty and land according to their family rights *(100 acres for the head of the family and 50 acres for each dependant)* as follows.

Name	Acres
Jean Louis Gibert	200
Anne Courneau Bouchonneau (Widow of Charles Bouchonneau)	150
Pierre Elie Belot	100
Jean Bellefaye	200
Joseph Bouchelon	150
Jean Baptiste Petie	150
Jean Roger	150
Pierre Reigne	150
Pierre Nicholas	150
Colas Bordajeau	300
Jean Bellot	250
Jean Baptiste de Laune	350
Jean Baptiste Gautier	250
Jean Lefaye	200
Marie Farasteau Gabau	150
Abram Jacob	250
Pierre Roquemore Ayne	250
Jacque Labruese	250
Jacques Langel	300
Jean Fresille	300
Jaque Boutiton	150
Anne Beraud Beinayme (Widow of Peter Beinayme)	150
Matthew Beraud	250
Daniel Louis Jennerett	100
Pierre Boutiton	100
Pierre Boutiton	100

The Huguenots of New Bordeaux

Francis Bayle	100
Pierre Leoron	100
Louis Villerett	100
Nicholas Basson	100
Antoine Billaw	100
Marie Magdale Belot	100
Jean Eymery	100
Marie Roger	100
Jeremiah Roger	100
Pierre Roger	100
Daniel Due	100
Theodore Gay	100
Jean Don	100
Jean Cartau	100
Jean Pierre Bellier	100
Pierre Garrineau	100
Nicholas Bouchonneau	100
Charles Bouchonneau	100
Anthoine Tanasteau	100
Andre Guillebeau	100
Francois Prouvillac	100
Jean Anthony	100
Jean Bouchilion	100
Marie Bayle	100
Cecile Bayle	100
Pierre Bayle	100
Jean Priolot	100
Jean Briau	100
Pierre Cluzzeau	100
Jean Audibert	100
Susanna Roquemore	100
Jean Pierre Roquemore	100
Anne Roquemore	100
Pierre Rolland	100
Francois Gros	100

Estienne Thomas	100
Marie Thomas	100
Susanna Latou	100
Anne Latou	100
Marthe Amnieu	100
Jean Dupuy	100
Pierre Langell	100
Jacque Langell	100
Jacob Baylard	100
Pierre Moragne	100
Matthiew Testall	100
Mathew Beraud	100
Jean Beraud du Conton	100
Pierre Pieron	100
Anny William	100
Philip Beard	100
Pierre Sudze	100
Joseph Labbe	100
Jacque Vallae	100
Jean Scervante	100

The Huguenot refugees arrived in South Carolina too late in the spring to plant provisions for their subsistence the ensuing winter on the lands they would eventually settle on. Consequently, the Governor and Council decided to send them to Fort Lyttleton, near Port Royal, some 50 miles to the south of Charles Town, probably by boat.

The refugees were temporarily housed in barracks and instructed to plant corn, peas, pumpkins, and potatoes for their subsistence. In addition, they were allocated one pound of flour and one quart of Indian corn for each person per day, and four steers each month for the whole group. In case of private disputes or difficulties they were instructed to contact Mr. De la Gay, a Frenchman who resided on Parris Island near Fort Lyttleton.

A few of the Huguenots separated from the main group early. A tailor, his wife and two children located in Charles Town. Fourteen people separated "through disgust or Quarrels" and were settled at nearby Purrysburg. And six men and their wives and children were settled elsewhere at the advice of the Council, because the wives had made a complaint which the Council thought "groundless and unreasonable:" that "the People who had Charge of distributing provisions had stop'd the rum from the Children which they had desired to be allowed to them instead of a Quantity of meat allowed them." [8]

A granite monument marks the site of the New Bordeaux Place of Worship.

Chapter Four

New Bordeaux Colony Founded

In the fullness of time, seeds sown in the blood-soaked soil of France gave birth to a Huguenot colony in the South Carolina back country. The refugees founded a town on Little River a half mile below its intersection with Long Cane Creek in present-day McCormick County, and a 28,000-acre township. Patrick Calhoun surveyed the land and nurtured and sustained the colony in its infancy. Calhoun had been instrumental in establishing the Long Canes Scots-Irish settlement nearby just eight years earlier and would later become the father of future senator, secretary of state, vice president, and statesman John C. Calhoun.

Lieutenant Governor William Bull named the town New Bordeaux, he said, for the city in France "from whence many of them came," and the township Hillsborough in honor of the Earl of Hillsborough, His Majesty's Principal Secretary of State for America.

The Huguenots of New Bordeaux

Bull instructed the Huguenots to select a committee of three deputies who would be provided with horses and a guide to travel into the back country to select land for their settlement. At the end of May 1764 the committee, headed by Pastor Pierre Boutiton, returned to Charles Town with their guide Patrick Calhoun. Pastor Boutiton reported back with three plats of different tracts of land, which were presented along with the request that the committee be allowed to "consult with the Colony" before making a final recommendation.

In a dispatch dated July 14, 1764, the lieutenant governor issued detailed instructions to Patrick Calhoun for establishing the Huguenot colony, which included a plan to create a town council to govern the colony. The plan directed establishment of a township for the refugees containing 28,000, with an allowance of 2,000 acres for several settlers who had already pioneered on portions of the land selected for the township. One of the settlers who had already staked out a 100-acre tract on Little River north of the New Bordeaux village was French Huguenot, Henry Breazeal.

Calhoun scheduled surveying of the land parcels in accordance with the order of land grants made on the April 18th.

In January 1765, Bull reported that nearly £600 had been expended, about £140 of it being paid out of the quit rents on order of the British Crown. At that time another £214 more was assigned for purchase of provisions for the colony.

Following is the text of Lieutenant Governor Bull's plan for the New Bordeaux colony.

I have given Commissn. Of Capt. To Mr. Due, Lieut. To Mr. Leoron, and Ensign to LeVoilett that they may do Militia Dutys by themselves and not be liable to Misunderstandings with Officers who cannot give their Order in a Language at present understood by the Colonists.

Some Persons with the Name of Commissary must be

chosen by them to take care of and Issue their Provisions once a Week at the rate of 1 lb. Of wheat flour or one quart of Indian Corn a day to each Person.

Upon there (their) arrival, as I hope you have executed my orders in purchaseing the Lands at the Fork (of Little River and Long Cane Creek) at a reasonable rate, you are to sett out 800 acres in a square for the Town in the following manner.

The Town to be Laid in 200, 1/2-acre Lotts and all Numbered is	100
For the Fort, Church Yard, parsonage in Town Market Place which will serve as a Parade, Public Mill, ea. 2 acre, and Land taken up in the Street will be about	25
For a Common, out of which must be reserved to the Government a right of granting 50 acres to make 100 more Lotts if the increasing of the Town renders it necessary	200
For a Glebe for a Minister of the Church of England	300
To be disposed of in 4 acre Lotts for the Cultivating their Vines and olives in the Infancy of this Colony, which They are very solicitous to obtain while they are afraid To go to their Plantations, these Garden Lotts to be Numbered	175

There shou'd be three or four roads Leading from the Town Laid out two or three miles whose Courses being known may prevent the Tracts being Cut in two by the roads to be run afterwards.

They are to build Houses in their Town, and a Fort, in it not Less than 120 feet quare of Palisades for their Common Security to which they may retire on any alarm and not abandon their Settlement, in which must be kept there (their) Store of Provision, arms, and ammunition.

As soon as these Works are almost finished, you are to

begin Surveying their Lands according to their Family Warrants to prevent Tummult and Confusion. In this work you are to begin running according to your Surveying Instructions. In the 1st Place for Mr. Roger, the Justice, 2nd Mr. Boutiton, the Minister, 3rd Capt. Due, 4th Lieut Lioron, 5th Ensign Le Violette, unless he gives his right to his Father, 6th The Commissary of Provisions, 7th The Physician, 8th Schoolmaster, if any after these the remainder are to take their turn by Ballan (ballot?), to be determined in presence of the 5 first named who are to serve as a council to the Colony in all difficulty Cases, and take order therein till the matter can be referred to the Govr. In Council for their future direction.

You are to purchase immediately a good Cow and Calf for every 5 Persons taking care that they are branded and marked in such a Manner to prevent disputes with any English Neighbour ... let their Horses also be branded.

A Public Mill ought to be Erected as soon as Conveniently Cou'd. They may be hunting (not looseing time from their Work) in Company of some rangers to procure some venison. This will save their money which their Eating of Beef will Consume too fast.

Pastor Gibert's Huguenot colonists returned to Charles Town after several months at Fort Lyttleton. Authorities contracted with Michael Smith, Jacob Bach, Martin Summerman, Nicholas Beekler, Thomas Grumblack, Andrew Houser, and Peter Bach to transport the refugees, their baggage and tools by wagon from Charles Town to the site of their settlement in the back country for £840.

Calhoun purchased 150 acres from James Davis for £250 for the village site. With the assistance of colonists, he platted boundaries and scaled in town lots, vineyard lots, and roads, and last surveyed and assigned plantation tracts.

Most of the men set out for New Bordeaux on July 17, 1764 "in great spirit" amid very rainy weather and floods. Only a few roads traversed the back country, which were no more than rough-cleared trails. About ten miles from Charles Town, they stopped for nearly a week because the horses were unable" to draw the Waggons forward" due to set, boggy roads. The second group set out either on the 18th or 19th of July. The remainder of the colonists, mostly women and children, remained in Charles Town."

The first group arrived to the east side of Little River near the site selected for New Bordeaux on August 5th. They cut down trees, and constructed a bateau to convey themselves and their effects across the river. The second group arrived two days later on August 7th.

The refugees immediately stored their arms and baggage in shelter that had been made ready for them on theDavis tract by Patrick Calhoun. Lieutenant Governor William Bull ordered a company of Rangers, at that time covering the Long Canes Scots-Irish and other settlers in the vicinity, to cover and assist the French Huguenot colonists on their settling. [1]

The fear of attack by hostile Indians remained. An attack by Cherokee Indians during the Cherokee War of 1760 had nearly wiped out the Long Canes settlement. And just the year before on Christmas Eve of 1763, Creek Indians skulked across the Savannah River and massacred fourteen people in the vicinity. [2]

Very soon after arrival the Huguenots began clearing land and cutting and logging timber to build family homes. By October 17th, they had six houses already set up and frames ready to erect fourteen more.

The remaining Huguenot refugees who had waited in Fort Lyttleton and then Charles Town more than six months, began departing during October. The first party reached New Bordeaux on November 14, 1764. For a while the colonists were plagued with boils and other ills, but three months later Calhoun wrote that they were recovered of their "indisposition."

The last group of settlers did not leave Charles Town

until January, with wagons carrying the weak and infirm. With this group went also vessels for brewing and silk making.

Patrick Calhoun wrote to Lieutenant Governor Bull, "The whole Town-ship may be said to abound with Hills, Springs & Vallies (altho in General plain enough for Tillige) with plenty of wild Game such as Deer, Turkeys &c. In the Learg Creeks are plenty of Fish, viz: Rock, shad, perch, Cate, Troute & c — at the lower End of ye glebe Land is a good Fish Dam formerly made by the Indians & since Repaired by ye white people. (Built of stones)"

The town of New Bordeaux was planned and built in the design typical of a French village on the sleepy stream called Little River. Log homes were built on half-acre lots in neat rows along narrow streets. On the home lots the Huguenot refugees planted vegetable gardens and fruit trees and bought livestock and fowl. Even now in springtime, the site reveals garlands of white blossoms of plum trees relevant to those French colonists of more than two centuries ago.

The French village was taking shape. Once situated in their new home, the Huguenots immediately put in place a local governmental council consisting of five members, the justice of peace, the minister, and the three officers of the village militia. New Bordeaux answered to the provincial government in Charles Town (the state capital) with the local governing council directing reports to the colonial assembly. The Justice of the Peace was supplied with a copy of Simpson's *Justices' Guide*. They organized a militia, to provide for an active and trained unit, which served as a defense against Indian attacks, and later for the cause of independence during the American Revolution.

The chatter of French-speaking refugees and the busy sounds of industry arose during the week, mingled with the fervent chanting of the once-interdicted psalms. Among a pious and devoted people, there were no idlers. Everyone had his appointed work, and on Saturday afternoon even the little children were seen, each with a wicker basket and snowy napkin, going and returning from the oven with loaves of bread.

The village was an all-inclusive community. Within the village there were the pastor, school teachers, and a medical doctor. There were skilled craftsmen: tailors, seamstresses, shoemaker, clog-maker, cabinet maker, coopers, wheelwrights, masons, carpenters, joiners, boatmen, vine dressers, and blacksmiths.

North of the village, on the southwest and northeast sides of Little River were the family, four-acre vineyard lots stretching along gentle slopes toward the river. On these mini-farms the Huguenots developed olive groves and grape vineyards. On the same lots they cultivated garden crops such as maize (Indian corn), potatoes, beans, and cabbage. And there were fruit trees scattered among the grape vineyards.

The saltus lands, that is the uncultivated lands, mostly forested in natural trees and vegetation, surrounded the village in great abundance. These lands they used for grazing their cattle, sheep, horses, goats, and hogs. And to the villagers these natural areas yielded a bonanza of resources such as fire wood, wild honey, berries, nuts, and any number of herbs for the cooking pot - dandelion, asparagus, and plenty of garlic. The saltus lands were replete with wild game, and the streams with fish.

Mary Elizabeth Moragne, a granddaughter of ship journalist Pierre Moragné, recorded, "In a short time a hundred houses had risen in a regularly compact body, in the square of which stood a building superior in size and construction to the rest, which served the threefold purpose of hotel, café house, and bureau des affaires for the little self-incorporated body. It was in a rich level valley, a few rods from the river, which they vainly supposed would furnish an easy access by navigation to remote places. The town was soon busy with the industry of its tradesmen; silk and flax were manufactured, whilst the cultivators of the soil were taxed with the supply of corn and wine. The hum of cheerful voices arose during the week, mingled with the interdicted songs of praise; and on the sabbath the quiet worshipers assembled in their rustic church, listened with fervent response to that faithful pastor who had been their spiritual leader through perils by sea and land, and who now directed their free, unrestrained devotion to the Lord of the forest."

Fort Bonne, was located adjacent to the village and vineyards on a ridge running from the hillside out to Little River and was surrounded with a palisade enclosure, which extended down to the river. The fort was in a "U" shape, with the east end of it being open and protected by the river and the north and south sides extending along the east side of the ridge and the west end was enclosed and surrounded the building. The purpose was to maintain a fort to which settlers could come in case of an Indian raid. The river provided a source of water in case of a siege. Also, the river afforded easier defense or retreat on that side.

Pierre Moragné wrote to his father still in France, "I commenced with two other persons to build us a (house); and in the month of February 1765, with the aid of God, I have begun to labor on my own land - on my half-acre, and afterwards on my four acres. The 13th of June I finished planting in corn and beans all the land, which I had been able to prepare. Though we have not a sufficiency yet we have enough to keep us from starving til our little harvest comes in. Towards the last of the month of July, we had an alarm created by the rumor that the Indians were coming to make wars upon us, and we all labored to dispose some trees so as to make a fort; but the rumor proved false"

The first recorded marriage in New Bordeaux was that of Pierre Moragné, son of Pierre and Marie Paris Moragné, to Cecille Bayle, daughter of Jean and Marie Seyral Bayle, on July 16, 1765 "after the publication of three banns." They were married by Monsieur Boutiton, Minister of the Gospel, with

New Bordeaux Colony Founded

Pierre Bellot and son Helie Bellot and other persons of the village of New Bordeaux in attendance.

Sixty more Huguenots, stranded in England for more than three years, joined the New Bordeaux colony on April 30, 1765. These refugees had fled from France because of religious persecution. Their petition to the Court of Saint James, dated May 28, 1762, stated, "That your Petitioners being in their native country deprived of the liberty of conscience, and persecuted for not conforming to the ceremonies of the Romish Church, have fled hitherto to seek refuge from their oppressors, and, under the protection of your Majesty's government, enjoy the blessings of civil and religious liberty. That your Petitioners, mostly bred to agriculture, have not hitherto been able to get employment, and thereby earn their living, but have been maintained principally by the charity of your Majesty's subjects.... (wish) an opportunity of settling in some of the British Colonies in America."

Claude Chabar sa femme & quatres Enfans. Laboureur de Terre
Pierre Boyan, Charpantier
Jean Jacques Gransar sa femme & quatres Enfans. Tisserand & Ouvrier de Terre
Paul Chauvet, Ouvrier de Terre
Claude Barnier, sa femme & un fils. Laboureur de Terre
Pierre Le Riche, sa feme & cinq Enfans. Tisserand
Jean Dron, sa feme & un Enfant. Tisserand
Jacques Chamberland. Jardiner & Boulanger
Claude Chauvet, sa feme & un Fils. Labourer de Terre & Fabriquant en Lame
Jean Pierre Blanchet & sa feme, Jardinnier
Jacques le Gros, sa femme & Quatres Enfans, Jardinnier
Pierre Chenton, Laboureur de Terre
Pierre Vaillant, Travailleur de Terre & Tailleur
Louis Salleri, sa femme & trois Enfans, Ouvrier de Terre

Matthieu Poitbin & sa femme, Laboureur de Terre
Jean Plisson, sa femme & un fils, Tisserand
Joseph Roulland & sa femme, Jardinnier & Ouvrier de Saltpetre
Jacques Paulet, Tonellier
Louis Marechal
Pierre Villaret & sa femme, Jardinier
Jean Beraud, Charpantier
Pierre Commer, Boulanger
Laurant Augustin, Boulanger
(A total of 60 persons)

Jacob Anger, a Huguenot colonist, petitioned the Council in 1765 for money to enable him to return to England and to slip back into France to arrange for his relatives to emigrate to New Bordeaux. Anger stated that he had left some twenty-five relatives in France who wished to join the New Bordeaux settlement. In his petition, Anger said that he was "afraid to write" for fear that his letters be intercepted in which case it would be "most detrimental to the family in France." The Council ordered disbursement in the amount of £100 currency to Anger for the mission.

The Reverend Jean Louis Gibert did not immediately settle at New Bordeaux, leaving the ministerial work to the Reverend Pierre Boutiton. Instead he devoted himself for the ensuing year, under the patronage of Gabriel Manigault, to raising silk on the site of the Cooper River near Charles Town. Pastor Gibert wasted no time making the right contacts in and around Charles Town to set the colony on the right course, and to establish the silk culture. Many in Gibert's flock came almost directly from the silk gardens of France and were well qualified to produce premium quality silk. Through his efforts the silk industry was promoted in New Bordeaux as well as the Charles Town area. He induced Gabriel Manigault of Charles Town to develop the industry there. During the first year after his arrival, he raised 620 pounds of cocoons on Manigault's plantation,

New Bordeaux Colony Founded

"Silk Hope," out of which he secured 50 pounds of drawn silk.

Pastor Gibert sailed for England with silk and cocoons to show to the London *inner circle* in an effort to secure financial support for building factories in South Carolina. The aid was readily given. An annual appropriation of £1,000 was appropriated for the extension of silk production in New Bordeaux and Charles Town. In 1766 or 1767 a factory for spinning silk was opened in New Bordeaux, as well as one in Charles Town. The product was shipped to England to be woven into cloth. The English, so anxious for successful silk production, waived the payment of duties on silk manufactured by the Huguenots and placed a bounty on its production and exportation to England.

The provincial government commissioned Pastor Gibert to teach the winding of silk and to supervise its production. Gibert secured three additional experts from France to assist in the new silk industry.

The *South Carolina-Gazette* for May 11, 1767, reported:

We have the pleasure to acquaint the public that the successful introduction of the SILK MANUFACTURE in this province bears a promising aspect as we hear there are great quantities of silk worms raised ... by the (New Bordeaux) French of Hillsborough and the English and Germans near Long Canes. Mr. John Lewis Gibert, a native of France, who is employed by the gentlemen concerned on behalf of the public in the encouragement of this manufacture, to wind and teach the winding of silk has now a considerable number of silk worms ... Workmen are now employed in building an oven for curing the cocoons, erecting four machines and all other necessaries for winding silk with all expedition.

By 1770 the Huguenot silk industry was progressing, but the thickening clouds of the American Revolution, and Gibert's untimely death at age fifty-one doomed the silk industry for New Bordeaux. The Reverend Jean Louis Gibert died in August 1773, from eating poisonous mushrooms. ₃

A nineteenth century writer penned, "A contrary wind, a long drought, a storm of sand – all these things have had their part in deciding the destinies of dynasties, the fortunes of races, the fate of nations. Leave the weather out of history, and it is as if night were left out of day, and winter out of the year." ₄

Contrary winds caused a group of colonists to join the already established settlement at New Bordeaux. ₅

Jean Louis Dumesnil de St. Pierre, a French Huguenot refugee living in London, conceived a plan to establish a colony in North America to cultivate a wine and silk industry on a commercial scale. He petitioned King George III for land to settle upon on March 9, 1765, stating in his petition that he could no longer live in France because he had been condemned to death for his perseverance in the Protestant religion, and for his inviolable attachments to the commercial interests of Great Britain. The British monarch approved the scheme and promised St. Pierre a land grant of 40,000 acres on Cape Sable Island near Halifax in Nova Scotia. Obviously, the king based his commitment on flawed information. Cape Sable Island is only two miles long. ₆

In Nova Scotia two decades earlier, Lord Edward Cornwallis had brought in a number of shiploads of British subjects to populate Halifax in competition with Louisbourg, a city of more than 4,000 French inhabitants founded in 1713 by France as its Gibralter in America for its ice-free port and cod fishery. The British seized Louisbourg in 1758. ₇

In 1765, St. Pierre was living on Dean Street in London. Before his exile, he had been master over extensive farm acres in Normandy, France, near Criqueville in Bessin and Port du Hoc in the vicinity of the World War II Allied D-Day invasion.

St. Pierre's colonists were selected about evenly between French and German Protestants skilled in growing grapes and fermenting wine to carry his plan forward. He likely recruited them in and around Spidalfields, his adopted neighborhood in London. Records indicate that some of the colonists or their ancestors had migrated through the French and German regions of Switzerland.

In at least one family in St. Pierre's group, the De la Chaux family, Jacob and Sarah Roberson Britt and their children, Charles Britt and James, there were members who had already migrated to Nova Scotia. Jacob's father Jean Nicolas De la Chaux and his father's brother and wife arrived in 1749 on the ship *Winchelsea*. Four-year-old Jacob had remained in Spidalfields in London with his mother, Jeanne Françoise Loup De la Chaux who was expecting the birth of another child. No doubt they now sought to join Jacob's father in Nova Scotia. Family ancestors had fled to Switzerland from France during the seventeenth century religious wars. [8]

This was an exciting period when the ships of leading nations could ply the ocean waters of the world. However, the weather elements posed a major adversary. The lack of instruments and the undeveloped state of science and hygiene in that age contributed to horrendous travel by sea. Many a ship, crew and passengers went to a watery grave because of lack of knowledge of climate and weather. Hurricanes and storms posed very significant threats. Ships traditionally sailed for the New World in the fall to avoid the normal hurricane season. Scurvy, a disease caused by the lack of vitamin C, took a terrible toll. Scurvy had puzzled physicians and philosophers since the time of the ancient Greeks.

Although the land grant on Cape Sable Island promised to St. Pierre for settling was in the same latitude as central France, temperature and precipitation differed markedly. In the realm of climatology, the region of Nova Scotia was subject to continental controls rather than to the maritime influences.

The climatic changes taking place in the northern hemisphere over the past millennia must be considered in relation to the Colonial period of settlement. Since the final glacial retreat from the mainland of North America about 10,000 years ago, several swings of the climatic pendulum have brought ever-changing temperature conditions. From a cold period at the end of the Middle Ages in the 1300s that firmly closed the sea access to Greenland and sometimes to Iceland, a brief warming period followed in the late 1400s and 1500s. Then a distinct thermal reversal followed, and the coldest temperatures since glacial times prevailed from the early 1600s for almost two centuries.

The period in time destined for the St. Pierre group to migrate occurred during the winter of 1767-68, one of the earliest and most severe winters on record in the British colonies. A temperature of 17° killed citrus trees at the British outpost of Pensacola in West Florida in January 1768. Ice was seen floating in the Mississippi River at Natchez, and at New Orleans ice formed several yards from the shore while the orange trees were killed. 9

After more than three years of preparation and anticipation, St. Pierre and perhaps 55 colonists boarded the brigantine *St. Peter* in the London harbor for a perilous voyage bound for Cape Sable Island in Nova Scotia – a destination none would ever reach. St. Pierre brought his wife, Marie Henrietta Hue de _quet and their infant daughter Henrietta Suzanne Victor.

The *St. Peter* drew her anchor free of the calm waters of the English Channel on September 26, 1767. The brigantine proceeded out onto the open seas. Once the sails were all set and the vessel was in good order, there was even time for the ship's crew to relax. The colonists fast lost sight of the coast and as the sun went down they were alone on the broad Atlantic.

Captain William Cawsey threaded the English sailing vessel on her way delicately between the whitecaps as the ship set out on the Atlantic Ocean, pushing her prow into the shallow

New Bordeaux Colony Founded

troughs of the sea running nearly due west. The captain skillfully kept abreast of their position at sea. The helmsman watched the needle of the astrolabe, a vital maritime instrument composed of loadstone imbedded in a float of cork that floated in its bath of oil and water. At night he sighted a star with the cross-staff. He used nautical charts to indicate position and a pair of dividers to trace the distance to the nearest shore and recorded latitude, longitude, course, and wind direction. Even with these inaccurate instruments, affected as they were by the roll of the ship on rough seas so that their usual error was as much as fifteen degrees, a skilled helmsman maintained a fairly accurate sense of location.

When not long at sea, the *St. Peter* began to encounter choppy waters. Increasingly brisk winds began to lash the vessel in this record-breaking early winter season. Hope for the winds to diminish faded. The weather continued to deteriorate. Eventually the brigantine was rolling furiously with the rising swells and running almost at right angles to their true course. Passengers worked tirelessly alongside the seamen at the pumps removing water from the hold of the leaky vessel. Seamen, lashed to the wheel, took turns at the helm. Great quantities of wind-swept water shook every timber in the ship and poured over the decks, threatening to totally engulf the passengers. High winds strained every rope and threatened to carry away every spar as well as the canvas; some of the sails were blown to ribbons. With every storm, the captain feared the ship's topmast was going and the ship broaching, which if it occurred the raging seas would capsize the vessel. All aboard clung to the ship and fought to keep it afloat for it was their only hope of survival.

As the weeks passed into months, one gale after another brought the fury of rain and hail and bitter-cold, winter winds. Captain Cawsey tried desperately to get the ship on a new tack so as to sweep the coast line of Newfoundland in order to reach Nova Scotia, but to no avail. The *St. Peter* was consistently driven southerly until they were hundreds of miles off course and not a great distance north of the Azores.

As it sailed, the *St. Peter* left in its wake a solemn graveyard across the wild high seas of the Atlantic. Ten of the colonists who died of scurvy en route were forever entombed in frigid watery graves.

By the first day of January 1768, the *St. Peter* was situated, "at latitude 41° north," according to St. Pierre's journal, his ship "being very leaky and the Colonists reduced to three pounds of bread for nine days and very sick of the scurvy, they did oblige (him) to bear and put into the harbour of Charles Town." [10]

For centuries the dreaded disease scurvy remained a major health hazard for seamen and passengers alike on long sea voyages because they had no means to carry fresh foods rich in vitamin C. Aboard ship for months at a time, voyagers consumed a diet deficient in the vital vitamin. Their food supply consisted primarily of biscuit and beef or pork. Scurvy is a hideous and frightful affliction by which the body's connective tissue degenerates, resulting in bleeding gums, wobbly teeth, rot-reeking breath, anemic lethargy, physical weakness, the opening of old wounds, and the separating of once healed broken bones. Although the bulk of scurvy-ridden victims usually recovered many succumbed to a slow, agonizing death. During the era, this most feared of all maritime diseases was responsible for more deaths on long sea voyages than storms, shipwreck, combat, and all other diseases combined. [11]

The helmsman steered the brigantine carrying the colonists toward Charles Town, South Carolina. Better weather prevailed. Nearly six weeks later, the *St. Peter* limped into the seaport on February 10, 1768, St. Pierre wrote, "after having been 138 Days at sea, in the greatest Distress,"

The surviving passengers refused "to put to sea again for any consideration, *n'est-ce pas!*"

In Charles Town, Lord Charles Montagu encouraged

New Bordeaux Colony Founded

St. Pierre to settle his Protestant colonists in the South Carolina back country with the French Huguenots at New Bordeaux. In compliance, St. Pierre was permitted to view the land of this district. St. Pierre visited the New Bordeaux settlement and found it entirely adapted to the colonists' plans for cultivating grape vines, silk and indigo agriculture. He is quoted as saying, "the New Bordeaux climate is about the same as the Marseilles, with a soil infinitely superior." [12]

Accordingly, the Commons House voted to award £1,197 to St. Pierre for the settlement of his group at New Bordeaux.

After hearing St. Pierre's request, the Commons House of Assembly granted lands in New Bordeaux as follows:

Name	Acres
Abram de Martile	100
Laurens Revere	100
Abraham Paw	150
Jacob de la Chaux	250
Johann Steifel	100
Johann Gerlogh Frick	250
Heinrich Drayer	200
Anna Dorothea	100
Elizabeth Deason	150
Robert Castle	100
Jean Du Vall	100
Elizabeth Forrester	100
Archibald Heynard	100
Peter Michl. LeRoy	200
Jean LeDue Depre	100
Ann Hugues	100
Heinrich Gasper	100
Robert Rogers	100
Thomas Goguett	100
Francis la Lande	100

James Sezor Boulonge	100
Francis Heller	100
Magdeline LeQuo	150
Jean Louis Demes'ne de St. Pierre	150

(A total of 37 according to family rights)

Lieutenant Governor Bull commissioned St. Pierre a Justice of the Peace and awarded him command of the militia of the New Bordeaux colony with the rank of captain.

Vine culture had been attempted in South Carolina earlier but not at any time had it been attempted upon so great a plan as that undertaken in 1768 by St. Pierre. He painstakingly set upon a scheme on a grand scale. His goal was to develop a wine industry in the back county of South Carolina that would rival that in France. St. Pierre advocated every planter in the district cultivating at least a half acre of grape vines. St. Pierre said an acre of vineyard ground commonly yielded from ten to twelve muids (Mwē) a year - a muid contained about 51 gallons.

St. Pierre ordered 1,574 plants from the Island of Madeira for the New Bordeaux colony. All of them thrived. One German in the colony produced 80 gallons of wine. The London Society for the Encouragement of Arts, Agriculture and Commerce awarded the German colonist 50 guineas for his success.

St. Pierre petitioned the Council July 12, 1769, for 20,000 French plants, "which Mr. De St. Pierre will provide or direct." In this petition St. Pierre states that they have had not only, "the necessaries, but the conveniences of Life; And Your Petitioners have not met with as much success as they could possibly expect in settling a great number of Vineyards," because of the "deficiency of Plants to carry on their Schemes so extensively as is necessary."

So confident of success, St. Pierre ordered 160,000 plants from French gardens, and invested his entire capital, save a patrimony in Normandy. He petitioned Lord Hillsborough, British Secretary of State for America, for £40,000. St. Pierre offered to mortgage all his lands and chattels in New Bordeaux. He proposed the incorporation of a joint stock company, which would sell shares at £50 each with a guaranteed interest at 6%. Under the proposed plan, the company would purchase slaves, machinery, and other capital items necessary for the success of the wine- making enterprise. St. Pierre appealed to Lord Hillsborough and other influential men in England to secure their support.

Government officials recommended that, "the Supervisors of the Silk Manufacture be directed to write Mr. John Delamore of London to procure from France such a quantity of Grape Cuttings and Plants as they should think necessary that the House do provide for the Expence thereof," and on the 11th following resolved that the sum of £700 be appropriated, "to procure from France a quantity of Grape Cuttings and Plants."

In June 1770, Lieutenant Governor Bull reported to Lord Hillsborough that most of the vines he "sent there (to New Bordeaux) last spring ... have taken root and the French and Germans may now contend for the honor of first introducing wine into the Province."

In 1771 Lieutenant Governor Bull sent up to New Bordeaux "a large Parcel of Vines lately arrived from the Island of Madeira."

On September 15, 1771, St. Pierre petitioned the British Crown for 20,000 acres in Georgia, "intending to promote the above branches of Agriculture as well in that Province as in Carolina, of which he is separated only by the River Savannah."

The following December, the Lords agreed to, "recommend to the King that St. Pierre be granted 5,000 aces in South Carolina."

St. Pierre's home, "Orange Hill," was on a beautiful site on a high knoll overlooking the Savannah River, with a panoramic view of Georgia beyond. It was located about four miles southwest of Willington. William Bartram, the Philadelphia botanist who spent the night of June 22, 1776, at Orange Hill gives the following information: "We lodged at the farm of Mons. St. Pierre, a French gentleman, who received and entertained us with great politeness and hospitality. The mansion-house is situated on the top of a very high hill near the banks of Savanna, overlooking his very extensive and well cultivated plantation of Indian Corn (Zea), Rice, wheat, Oats, Indigo, Convoloulus Batata, &c., these are rich low lands lying very level betwixt these natural heights and the river; his gardens occupy the gentle descent on one side of the mount, and a very thriving vineyard, consisting of about five acres, is on the other side."

Sometime during 1771, St. Pierre returned to England to secure superior plants from France, and to recruit additional trained vine dressers. His Memorial to the Lords of the Treasury, February 20, 1772, states, "he has already at the Expence of his whole little Fortunes established and brought to perfection the growing and making of silk, the Culture of Vines, and the making of Wine, at New Bordeaux, and that the Honourable Society for the Encouragement of Arts, Manufactures, and Commerce have, in testimony of their intire approbation, given a Premium of Fifty pounds Sterling for the Wine already produced, and were also pleased upon the 15th of January last (1772) to honour your Memorialist (St. Pierre) with a Gold Medal in that he had established and brought to perfection the growing and making of silk, the culture of vines and the making of wine, at New Bordeaux."

While in England, St. Pierre published a 344-page book entitled *The Art of Planting and Cultivating the Vine*. A translation of St. Pierre's book is preserved in the United States Library of Congress. Following is an excerpt.

White Wine

The best grapes used for making white wine are the Melier, the Beaume, and the Fomenter. They must be gathered towards the close of the vintage, must be of the red sort, be trodden in the vat, which is reserved for white grapes, taking care to have the press well washed before the Marc or husks are pressed, lest it take a red tinge. As white wines are subject to turn yellow when badly managed, to avoid this inconvenience, we must by no means suffer them to ferment. White grapes, in order to yield a very clear wine must be taken out of the vat almost as soon as put into it and be immediately put into the press, where indeed they are most commonly unloaded, directly as they come from the Vineyard, and put into casks, as they are preserved.

St. Pierre told officials, "the Settlement at New Bordeaux doth now consist of about one hundred and ten French Protestant settlers; that your Memorialist now has one hundred thousand vine plants (Exclusive of Sixty thousand already sent by the Carolina Packet to New Bordeaux) and above twenty families of French Protestants, all Vine Dressers, now ready to embark with him for New Bordeaux," but before he could increase the Colony by this number," he asked for £4,200 to carry his plan into execution. As part of his effort to influence the British government to furnish this financial aid, St. Pierre submitted, on the 16th of March 1772, a detailed report of his observations. [13]

But, Lord Hillsborough suddenly reversed his position from the resolute support he had previously given the New Bordeaux colony saying that although the Commissioners of Trade and Plantation felt that St. Pierre's settlement had been undertaken and carried on with great spirit and activity and could not fail, "of being usefull to this Kingdom in the Production of those Articles of Consumption, which are now principally imported from foreign Parts that they had done all which in the present state of this Business, it was fit for them to do."

St. Pierre was stunned and disappointed over loss of further financial aid and was at a loss to know why Lord Hillsborough pulled support; he said that, "although the Noble Lord's not vouchsafing me his countenance - was an unexpected mortification, yet did not suffer it to damp my spirit nor to make me remit my assiduity."

Some friends of high rank in England came to St. Pierre's aid, even though the government there did not. They subsidized the cost for transporting additional French and German Protestants to join St. Pierre's wine industry. The colonists arrived in South Carolina on December 21, 1772.

The emigrants were granted bounty land in New Bordeaux as follows:

Name	Acres
Theodore Brewer	200
Johann Bennet Slater	100
Mathias Cor	200
Gear Lad Metager	250
Arnuldus Rougimont	200
Nicholas la Fille	100
Will Saller	200
Peter Gaillard	100
Heinrich Abraham Shultz	200
Johann Willingham	100
Jacole Pfeiffer	300
Johann Barchinger	100
Wilhelm Pfaff	300
Martif Ruppel	250
Claude Gaillard	100
Lour Loram Lartege	100
Heinrich Jager	100
Wilhelm Hook	100

Stephen Jeachin	100
Jean Miolett	100
Jean Gottier	100
Georg Tobert	200
Samuel Steinoch	100
Jean Jacques Masle	100
Johann Sneider	100
Rosina Enharding	100
Barbara Enharding	100

(A total of 53 persons according to family rights) [14]

St. Pierre probably never learned why Lord Hillsborough turned his back on New Bordeaux's aspiring wine industry. Records reveal that loss of backing from the British Crown derived from international politics and greed.

When news of St. Pierre's far-reaching plans for wine production reached France, the French government and wine makers were furious. France, having felt the sting of England's colonial encroachment on her industries, was alarmed. Wine makers in France felt threatened and humiliated by the success and scope of St. Pierre's wine producing endeavor in New Bordeaux, South Carolina. Prominent Frenchmen such as Guillaume Raynal and Marquis Chastellux strongly protested. The French government sent a stiff manifesto to London stating that, "wine culture should be left to France and France alone."

In addition, the French government secretly delivered a £50,000 bribe to Lord Hillsborough, British Minister to the American Department, to induce him to withdraw support from the New Bordeaux wine industry.

The interference of the French government, the £50,000 bribe paid to Lord Hillsborough, and finally the developing American Revolution interrupted the development of St. Pierre's marvelous venture for the culture of the grape that held such promise for the Huguenot colony. [15]

Even before the Huguenot refugees had left Charles Town in 1764, Lieutenant Governor Bull appointed officers for a military company so, "that they may do Militia Duty by themselves": Captain Daniel Due, Lieutenant Pierre Leoron, and Ensign La Violette.

In 1771, St. Pierre was captain of this company. While in England in 1772, he petitioned the Lords Commissioners of Trade and Plantations for "one hundred and fifty musquets for the defence of him and his Settlers against the Indians." On January 14, 1773, Lord Charles Montagu appointed St. Pierre a lieutenant of Fort Charlotte, a stone fort constructed in 1765-66 on the Savannah River at a point a few miles up-river from New Bordeaux for protection of the settlers in the area against warring Cherokee and Creek Indians. The post was garrisoned primarily by New Bordeaux Huguenots and Long Canes Scots-Irish.

Trouble with the Cherokee Indians returned to the back country in 1776 in conjunction with Great Britain's naval attack on Fort Sullivan at Charles Town. The Cherokee Nation allied with the British during the American Revolution.

Closely coordinated with their naval assault, British officials ordered Agent John Stuart to have the Cherokees ready for a concentrated attack on the back country. Upon the British move onto Charles Town, runners headed up the Cherokee Path to give the signal to the Indians.

On July 1st, Cherokee warriors swarmed down upon unsuspecting settlers in the back country. A war party dashed into the Long Canes, only a few miles from New Bordeaux, and murdered several members of the Aaron Smith family. John Smith, though wounded, galloped to White Hall (south of present-day Greenwood) to inform Major Williamson.

Major Williamson called out the Ninety Six Regiment of militia. By August 1st, the regiment was marching toward the Cherokee Nation. The regiment included militiamen from New Bordeaux, the Long Canes, and the German settlement, Londonborough on Hard Labor Creek. Officers included Jean Louis du Mesnil de St. Pierre of New Bordeaux, and Andrew

New Bordeaux Colony Founded

Pickens and James McCall of the Scots-Irish Long Canes.

The militia regiment invaded the Cherokee Nation. Militiamen defeated the Cherokees in 5 battles, burned 32 of their towns and villages, and scorched their valleys, destroying crops of corn, orchards, and livestock.

St. Pierre was killed in a battle near Essenacca in the Cherokee Lower Towns.

Many young Cherokee warriors migrated westward. The older chiefs sued for peace. On May 20, 1777, a delegation of Cherokee headsmen met commissioners from South Carolina and Georgia at Dewitt's Corner (Due West). In order to obtain peace and resume normal trading, the Cherokees ceded their lands east and south of the Appalachian Mountains. [16]

St. Pierre's death was a blow to the New Bordeaux colony. Wine making on a much smaller scale continued in the colony well into the nineteenth century, but it would never return to the grand scale of the era of the master of the vineyard.

During the Revolutionary War, New Bordeaux colonists served as a company, commanded by Matthew Béraud. The New Bordeaux company fought in the Battle of Ninety Six where the first blood of the American Revolution in South Carolina was shed in November 1775.

Matthew Béraud was killed at the Siege of Savannah, October 9, 1779. Subsequently, Joseph Bouchillon became captain. Jean David, Pierre Gibert, and Pierre Roger served as lieutenants. Non-commissioned officers and enlisted men included: Jean Audebert, Jacob Baylard, Pierre Bellot, Jean Bellotte, Pierre Bordajeau, Robert Calder, Jean Chamberland, Lazarus Covin, F. Rene LeRoy Ducerqueil, Antoine Gabeau, Pierre Garrineau, André Guillebeau, Pierre Moragné, Pierre Moragné Jr., Benjamin Petit, and Pierre Sudre. Charles Bouchineau served as a clerk in the General Department of Purchases, Jean Castine served as a captain in Colonel Hammond's Regiment. [17]

New Bordeaux colonists served the Patriot cause, being

Whigs to the last man. They suffered greatly from continual depredations by Tories. Pierre Moragné, in attempting to rescue a fine horse that the Tories were stealing from his stables, received a gunshot wound in the leg that disabled him for life. A slave girl, stolen and conveyed to the Cherokee Indians, was rescued several years later. Lieutenant Pierre Roger sometimes made a hasty visit to his family but seldom obtained a night's rest, being compelled instead to make his dwelling in a swamp near his home.

Often the Huguenot women and children had to take refuge in Fort Charlotte on the Savannah River, Fort Cowen near Little River or Fort Engevine on the east side of Little River opposite the village. Sometimes they clubbed together in homes for mutual encouragement and protection against the pillaging foes. The Tories took horses, food, and even the blankets from sleeping children. The Huguenot women secretly stored provisions on an island in the Savannah River. [18]

Of the schools taught by the teachers of the New Bordeaux colony little is known. A school teacher, Antoine Joseph Labbe migrated in the first group of refugees with Pastor Gibert.

Although he did not bring teachers in his group, St. Pierre did not neglect the education of his colonists. George Wilks, who came to South Carolina from England about June 1768, was soon after employed by St. Pierre "to keep a school" in Hillsborough Township. His tract of 100 acres was surveyed April 1, 1769, and granted July 28, 1769. Just how long Mr. Wilks taught there is not known.

Jean Jacques Noble conducted a school during the early period.

By 1785, the colonists in and about New Bordeaux had by subscription erected a Grammar School (French and English) with Pierre Gibert as school master. The following is his interesting announcement TO THE PUBLIC:

"The French Protestant Settlement in and about New

New Bordeaux Colony Founded

Bordeaux, Ninety Six district, whose exertions in support of our independence are well known, having by subscription erected a French and English Grammar School, on a plan approved of and countenanced by Gentlemen of the first note, and having appointed the subscriber Master of the said School, he begs leave to inform the public, that he proposes to take in pupils at the price of Ten Guineas per annum (to be paid quarterly) for boarding, washing, and tuition. The advantage of acquiring at so easy a rate, this useful as well as polite branch of education, in a part of this State, which for healthfulness of the air, and excellence of winter, may with propriety have been named Montpellier, must be obvious, and the subscriber makes no doubt, but that, as nothing but French is in common spoke in his family, his pupils will be able to speak it with some propriety in the course of one year. His moral character and deportment, and his whole family, he flatters himself, will bear the strictest security. He will pay particular attention to the morals as well as politeness of his pupils - and Mrs. Gibert (Elizabeth Bienamè) to their cleanliness."

The next noted teacher in or near New Bordeaux was Dr. Moses Waddel. In 1801, he removed from Columbia County, Georgia, to Vienna, where he opened a school that year. Vienna, sister city to Petersburg, was located on the Savannah River about five miles southeast of present-day Mt. Carmel. The following year, 1802, he accepted a call to Hopewell Church, becoming as many ministers of that day did, both a pastor and a teacher. At the request of the French Huguenots at New Bordeaux and the Scots-Irish in the Long Canes, Waddel removed from Vienna to Willington - midway between Vienna and New Bordeaux - and began the school, which later made him one of the most noted teachers South Carolina has ever known. As a result of an agreement between leading citizens of the community and the Trustees of the Vienna Academy, the school building in Vienna, which was begun in 1801, but which had not been completed because of lack of funds, was removed to Willington, and was converted into a convenient house of worship and an academy building - all under one roof. The congregation worshiping there was formally organized into Willington Presbyterian Church in 1809. Moses Waddel developed the school into the Willington Academy, a notably competent prep school that introduced boys to the life of the mind, taught them very strict Calvinistic self-discipline, and schooled them so well in the texts of the time as to be called the South's greatest educator. [19]

Pictured is the grave marker for Huguenot refugee Pierre Moragné, ship journalist aboard the Friendship.

Plat of New Bordeaux and Hillsborough Township, surveyed by Patrick Calhoun for the French Huguenots, 1765.

Pierre Boyer Moragné House. Destroyed by fire in 1971.

André Guillebeau House, now preserved in Hickory Knob State Park.

New Bordeaux Colony Founded

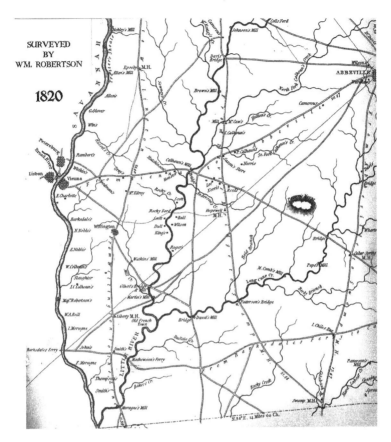

Portion of a map of Abbeville District surveyed by William Robertson in 1820 shows the site of New Bordeaux as "Old French Town" on Little River just below intersection with Long Cane Creek, and related sites including Liberty Meeting House, Willington, Fort Charlotte, Vienna, Petersburg, and Lisbon.

Chapter Five

Assimilation

The rapid and relatively smooth assimilation of the New Bordeaux Huguenots into the English-speaking South Carolina back country is a remarkable occurrence. While they did not assimilate overnight the process occurred rather quickly.

It is obvious that the colonists remained in England long enough to be well acquainted with the Anglican principles and to learn the essentials of Anglicanism as to worship, form of government, and doctrines. The experience likely benefitted them to an extent sufficient to break down many of their prejudices. As a result they were able to conform to the prevailing order present in a region populated primarily by Scots-Irish people. The absorption of the Huguenots extended to customs, to language, to proper names, and even to blood.

Assimilation

For whatever reason there was often a desire to become anglicized. Therefore, some people changed their surnames completely, others modified them, still others accepted the English equivalent. In some cases surnames simply took on an English pronunciation in the new English-speaking culture. For example, *Bordajeau* became Birdashaw, *De la Chaux* became Dillashaw/Dilleshaw/Delashaw, *LeRiche* became Richey/Richie, *Roger* became Rogers, *Chamberland* - Chamberlain, *Labrousse* - Labruce. *LeRoy* sometimes took the equivalent King.

Change in given names was widespread, too. *Jean* was anglicized to John, *Jeanne* to Jane, *Pierre* to Peter, *Françoise* to Frances, *François* to Francis, *Philippe* to Philip, *Marguerite* to Margaret, *André* to Andrew, *Suzanne* became Susan, *Antoine* - Anthony, *Étienne* - Stephen, *Jacques* - Jacob or James, *Louis* - Lewis, *Marie* - Maria, *Matthieu* - Matthew, *Cécile* - Cecilia, *Henri* - Henry. Thus, with their English veneer many of the names are today hardly recognizable.[1]

Within one or two decades there was considerable intermarriage with neighbors of Scots-Irish and English nationalities. Both of Pastor Jean Louis Gibert's daughters married outside their French culture to *Scots-Irish* farmers in the Long Canes settlement.

After Pastor Gibert's death in 1773, his widow Jeanne Boutiton, moved their children Louise, Jeanne, and Joseph to Charleston, where she met and married merchant Pierre Engevine, a fellow immigrant and native of Bordeaux, France. Pierre was able to introduce his stepchildren to many of the amenities and advantages of urban life. When Jeanne died in 1783, Pierre gave up his business to take his stepchildren back to Badwell, the family farm at New Bordeaux. There he built a new house and began to cultivate the land the children had inherited from their mother. Louise married dashing William Pettigrew. She, with younger sister Jeanne, moved several miles to William's farm in remote Flat Woods into a cabin on White's Creek with *only two ground-floor rooms and a loft*, which they occupied for twelve years. With Jeanne's inexperienced support, Louise bore the first of her nine children. Jeanne married Thomas Finley, William's close friend and only near neighbor. When Jeanne died in 1795, Louise adopted infant Louis Finley. Fonder of fishing, hunting, and horse racing than farming, William soon stumbled into debt. Stripped of his farm by his creditors, William moved his pregnant wife and their four boys to the Gibert family farm in 1800. There, propertyless and humiliated, he merged his household with that of Louise's peculiar, bachelor brother, Joseph, who occupied Badwell after both his sisters married. At two-to-three year intervals, she bore the rest of her children. [2]

Pierre and Elizabeth Bienaime Gibert parented six sons and five daughters. Of the three sons who married, only one took a wife from the French community. All five daughters married, and not one married within the French community. [3]

In the second and third generations, marriage outside the French culture was widespread. Examples include: *Isaac Moragné* who married Margaret Blanton Caine, *Pierre Francis Moragné* married Mary Ann Todd, *Pierre Boyer Moragné* - Amanda Rachel Allen, *Mary Elizabeth Moragné* - William Hervey Davis, *Francis Moragné* - Jane Taylor, *Archibald Breazeal* married Dorcas Watson, *Eliza Rogers* married Jesse Dabbs, *Eliza Rogers* - John Harbuck.

Leonard Martin married Catherine Lazenby, *John Martin* - Mary Barksdale, *Sarah Martin* - James Calhoun, *Stephen Gibert* married Sarah Pettigrew, *Dr. Joseph Gibert* - Jane Terry, *Elizabeth Gibert* - Stephen Lee, *Harriet Gibert* - Joseph Hillhouse, *Lucy Gibert* - Benjamin Kennedy, *Drusilla Gibert* - William Houston.

Nancy Breazeal married Robert McLinton, *John Chamberlain* married Rebekah Cook, *Peter Covin* married Delilah Bryan, *Susan Covin* - James Thomson, *Elizabeth Covin* - John Clay, *Jacob Dillashaw* married Jane Weeks, *Elizabeth Dillashaw* - Samuel Mann, *Peter Dilleshaw* - Mary Catherine

Assimilation

Graham, *Catherine Deleshaw* - Ellis Carrol, *Jacob Belot* married Sarah Dickson, *Peter LeRoy* married Anne Beattie, *Amanda Bouchelle* married William F. Shields, *Lazarus Guillebeau* married Marcella Palmer, *James Leonard Bouchillon* married Delilah America Shirley.

Even before departing for the New World, refugee Jacob De la Chaux had taken an English wife, Elizabeth Roberson Britt, in London. [4]

French was still spoken in the homes by second generation Huguenots. It is recorded that William Pettigrew came home one evening from work tired and moody, to find his wife, Louise (Pastor Gibert's daughter) entertaining an itinerant Frenchman. For some time at the chimney corner he sat silent and morose. The stranger at length endeavored to engage him in conversation with the remark,

"Mais, Monsieur, vous parlez Français?"

"No, sir," replied Pettigrew, "I speak no French and very little English!" [5]

Pierre Gibert stated in 1785 that only French was spoken in their home. [6]

Mary Elizabeth Moragné, granddaughter of ship journalist Pierre Moragné, read French fluently, having a background in it at home, she said, since her father, Isaac Moragné, had spoken nothing else until age twelve. [7]
Certainly by the turn of the century, French had become a second language in the Huguenot community.

A tragic event in the early French community testifies to the perplexity of adapting to an unfamiliar environment, which resulted in the death of Pastor Jean Louis Gibert. Jean LeRoy prepared mushrooms for the pastor's dinner from an unknown American variety that resembled a common, edible French one. The mushrooms were poisonous. The pastor became ill and died in a matter days in August 1773 at age fifty-one. [8]

Pierre Gibert, a son of Pastor Jean Louis Gibert's brother Pierre, played a pivotal role during the assimilation of the Huguenots into the whole community. Later called Peter Gibert, he immigrated to the New Bordeaux colony about 1771. He served as a school master for many years and a religious leader during his adult life. Fluent in English as well as his native French, his education proved highly useful in dealing with the Scots-Irish and English settlers already in the area and also the legal and political sector of the French community particularly in translating wills, deeds, and other documents from the French. Pierre Gibert married Elizabeth Bienaime who had immigrated at age four with the original refugees in 1764. An extensive planter, his plantation would eventually grow to 1400 acres. Peter Gibert was instrumental in persuading Moses Waddel to move his famous academy from Vienna to Willington and was a leader in the Willington Presbyterian Church where he served as an elder. He served as a magistrate, several terms in the South Carolina General Assembly, and as a trustee of the estate of John de la Howe for the creation of Lethe, now John de la Howe School. 9

Contrary to the French Huguenot communities established a century earlier along the tide-water area of South Carolina, which were practically forced into allegiance with Anglicanism, ecclesiastical assimilation into the English-speaking back country played out differently for the New Bordeaux refugees. Existing factors contributed to this development. First, the majority of the New Bordeaux refugees' neighbors were Scots-Irish Presbyterians in the Long Canes settlement. Also, there were no Anglican churches in the immediate area.

The New Bordeaux refugees deviated from the game plan set by King George III. Instead of their British benefactors' planned Church of England, the New Bordeaux refugees established a church of the Calvinistic faith. During the infancy of the village, Reverend Pierre Boutiton held divine services in the log building that served as the town hall or "bureau des affaires" on the square. Lieutenant Governor Bull wrote on

Assimilation

November 30, 1770 that, "between the Congarees, the Indian Boundary, and Saludy River ... there are no less than six meeting houses built and ministers maintained by the poor Inhabitants, besides those of the French Protestants at Hillsborough and the German Lutherans in Londonburg, and not one church of England congregation." At this period in time, settlers on the frontier frequently did not worship in *churches per se*, but as *organized congregations* they held their services in multi-purpose *meeting houses*. The Huguenots might have opted for the town hall for worship to avoid the King's mandated Church of England.

A petition in 1771 to the Commons House requested that a church, "be built at New Bordeaux, and a Sum of Money allowed for the support of a Clergyman to preach the Gospel among them, in the English and French Languages." Records do not indicate whether funds were appropriated for raising a church building.

After the death of Pastor Boutiton, St. Pierre petitioned the Board of Trade in London in 1772 to provide funds for another pastor. The annual sum of £50 had been given by the Society for the Propagation of the Gospel. St. Pierre requested that the appropriation be continued, and recommended calling Rev. Peter Levrier to serve the Huguenots in New Bordeaux. Rev. Levrier had been pastor of the church at Pensacola in British Florida for the past seven years. The request was granted. Rev. Levrier arrived at Charles Town in May 1772, bound for his new charge in New Bordeaux.

The government granted the allowance, and on July 17, 1772, ordered that, "15 French Bibles and 36 French Prayer books and psalms, and 50 of Lewis' Catechisms in French be sent," for the use the Huguenots. Pastor Levrier demitted the charge November 20, 1772.

As the colony advanced, the restricted limits of the village of New Bordeaux were found too narrow, and the colonists dispersed more widely to their farms in the adjoining country. The place of worship was removed from the village to the site of Fort Bonne on the banks of Little River. Here they conducted their simple service without a pastor, the reading of sermons and singing of psalms being conducted chiefly by Pierre Moragné, the prayers by Pierre Gibert.

During the Reverend Robert Mecklin's ministry, followed by Dr. Cummins's, at Hopewell Presbyterian Church in the Long Canes, many of the Huguenots walked 10 miles to that church where they mingled and worshiped with the Scots-Irish. "It was affecting," said one of their number, "to see them meet at this place, always saluting each other with a kiss, while tears flowed down their checks." Two pews were reserved for their use. One of their number, Pierre Gibert, was elected elder to represent them in session. Huguenots worshiped at Hopewell for more than 20 years.

The Huguenots eventually opted for a more convenient and advantageous location. In 1796, their attention was called to a missionary, the Reverend John Springer who traveled through the neighborhood on his way to a station, probably Ninety-Six. Springer was formerly president of the college at old Cambridge, but now a resident of Georgia. He accepted the call to preach once a month in a small log school house near a fine spring directly on this road from Barksdale Ferry, and within a mile of the village of New Bordeaux.

Springer's labors inspired serious people of all denominations who ultimately agreed to build a house of worship. They called it "Liberty Meeting House," implying that any orderly minister should have admission to preach in it. Upon the death of the Reverend Springer in 1798, the seed sown by the wayside was not left to perish. Scots-Irish Reverend Moses Waddel, also a member of Hopewell presbytery at that time, followed soon in the footsteps of the faithful missionary, and cheered the hearts of the Huguenots by the efforts of his youthful zeal. Early in the nineteenth century, a suitable frame building was erected at this spot. Many of those who had joined

Assimilation

Hopewell, transferred their membership to this place, and Pierre Gibert and Pierre Moragné, junior, were elected elders. Not satisfied with only the itinerant labors of Moses Waddel, the people obtained a regular appointment for the third Saturday and Sabbath in each month.

Then in 1809, Waddel, who was then living in Willington, organized Willington Presbyterian Church for them and for others in the community.

Church affiliation of the Huguenots extended into the community to Buffalo Baptist Church, Lodimont and Mt. Carmel Presbyterian churches, and Mt. Tabor Methodist Church. [10]

Most of the Huguenot refugees were poor and homeless yet thrifty, sturdy, industrious, and cultured. By all means they were not a helpless horde destined to poverty. No evidence was found to suggest any disfavor toward the Huguenots from their English-speaking neighbors in the social, economic or political realms. Indeed, South Carolina profited materially by giving these thrifty refugees a home on her soil. In turn, the soil served the colonists well. Farms and plantations were soon established. Men, women and children labored almost unceasingly to improve their station in life in pursuit of the American idea of merit and hard work for attaining success, not hereditary privilege. In the succeeding generations, these people and their descendants excelled and contributed enormously in the varied realms of society.

The refugees had no problem with labor. In France the mass of them had been of the middle class, tillers of the soil, artisans, craftsmen, laborers, etc. In New Bordeaux it became necessary to clear the forest for cultivation and erecting houses.

King George III and his Lords financed and promoted the settling of the New Bordeaux colony primarily for the purpose of establishing the cultivation of grapes, silk, and olives. In the infancy of the village of New Bordeaux, families cultivated garden crops, corn, grape vineyards, and olives on their 4-acre vineyard lots. They produced vegetables, milk, pork, beef, eggs, etc. for home consumption. During the first decade there was serious pursuit of a silk industry as well as cultivation of grapes and wine production on a commercial scale, which showed great promise of success prior to the American Revolution.

The tumultuous Revolutionary War left a region desolate and destitute. By its end the South Carolina back country was adorned with farms overgrown with weeds and depleted of crops and livestock, and populated by a tremendous number of widows and orphans and men maimed and disabled from battlefield injuries. Nowhere else in America was there a more ravaged countryside and such fratricidal horror as that experienced by the back country population.

In the aftermath of the war and quest for new order in the young nation there was drastic change in the economic sector. Slavery was evident in the area from the beginning but during the early years of the New Bordeaux colony there were not many slaves present. The majority could neither afford to own slaves nor did they have the need. Early on a livelihood was closely interlocked with ownership of livestock and fowls along with tobacco, flax, and indigo as money crops. Cotton was grown on the scale of a garden crop only since it was time-consuming to produce lint by hand. But, a new system of farming would soon emerge. *11*

After the Revolutionary War considerable out migration became widespread as many refugees moved away to Charleston and west and south to other states and territories, and the colonists began to relocate to their large tracts of land to build farms and plantations out in the township, which together greatly reduced the population in the village of New Bordeaux.

Mary Elizabeth Moragné described the demise of the French village in poetic verse published in *The Female Prose Writers of America*, "Did I say there was no beauty there? — None but the clear glancing of the rippling stream, and the high

Assimilation

arching of the solemn woods above, wreathing their limbs in fantastic forms against the deep blue sky, and forming a natural temple, in which each tree stood up tall and distinct as a polished shaft in the midst. The solemn elm, and deep green river oak were there, sustaining the slender larch, and twining their branches through the light-green foliage of the maple, which beautifully contrasted the glittering notched leaves of the fragrant gum. The woods still wave on in melancholy grandeur, with the added glory of near a hundred years; but they who once lived and worshiped beneath them - where are they? Shades of my ancestors - where? No crumbling wreck, no mossy ruin, points the antiquarian research to the place of their sojourn, or to their last resting-places! The traces of a narrow trench, surrounding a square plat of ground, now covered with the interlacing arms of hawthorne and wild honeysuckle, arrest the attention as we are proceeding along a strongly beaten track in the deep woods, and we are assured that this is the site of the 'old French town,' which has given its name to the portion of country around. After some years, but not till the country was established in peace, it was gradually abandoned ... to move out upon the hills, to which their familiarity with the usages of the country had now rendered them less opposed; and it must be confessed, also, that in the course of the Indian wars, and the scenes of the revolution which followed, attrition with the more enterprising and crafty had worn off so much of their native simplicity as to admit the passion of avarice, which, by calling them to a more enlarged sphere, greatly tended to the oblivion of their town, though more than half a century had passed away before they had forfeited any of their national characteristics, or admitted any corruption of their native tongue." [12]

    In a speech celebrating the 90th anniversary of the arrival of the French Huguenots to New Bordeaux, William Caine Moragné said, "The site of the town was selected, doubtless, with the view to the navigability of the stream and the adaptation of the soil to the culture of the vine; for our fathers, coming from the south of France, had experience in vine-dressing, and were not without knowledge of the blessings of commerce: though, at this distant period of time, we can but wonder at the short-sighted policy, which prompted them to reject the sunny hills and fertile valleys, and smooth current of the Savannah for the more damp and inhospitable region of this now sluggish stream."

However, in retrospect it is doubtful that the choice to locate the village on Little River rather than on the Savannah River four miles away actually made any appreciable difference as far as the survival of New Bordeaux as a village or town. There were so many other contributing factors, which actually led to its demise.

In comparison, a generation after New Bordeaux was founded, Vienna and sister-cities Lisbon and Petersburg sprang up a few miles north on either side of the Savannah River and flourished to regional importance early in the nineteenth century only to experience the same fate. The trade centers served as a cartelist on the navigable river for shipping tobacco, flour, and cotton and for receiving products needed by area farm and plantation citizenry. After a generation of prosperity westward migration reduced Vienna, Lisbon, and Petersburg to ghost towns. Progressive America was on the move.

Two landmark events clinched the production of short staple cotton - the invention of a workable cotton gin by Eli Whitney in 1793, then Augusta, Georgia inventor Hogden Holmes' much-improved gin in 1796. Whitney's intention to corner the market on the manufacture of the cotton gin failed. Right away blacksmiths were bypassing patent rights and mass-producing cotton gins.

The world had never seen a better place to grow cotton than the South. Farmers quickly turned cotton from mostly a garden crop to a commodity. The climate was right, the soil rich, and black slaves were available to supply the immense amount of labor needed to cultivate it. Cotton almost instantly reigned

Assimilation

king and the economy of the South became wrapped up in cotton, land, and slaves. *13*

Historians have pondered the moral logic of Huguenots becoming slaveholders. Census records reveal that the New Bordeaux Huguenots, like their neighbors, were quickly drawn into the stream of slave-hungry purchasers with the crowning of "King Cotton." Even though the number of colonists remaining in New Bordeaux had dwindled greatly, by 1800 the small number of Huguenot planters in the community held at least 85 slaves. Production of cotton on a large scale depended upon land and slaves. Cotton brought wealth. Slaves often accounted for more than 80% of the value of a planter's worth.

Even political aspirations were tied to owning land and slaves. Election of a representative to the South Carolina General Assembly required ownership of a minimum of 550 acres of land and 10 slaves; election as a senator twice that. *14*

Early in the nineteenth century as slavery became an issue, the planter elite moved the discussion away *from race to class* by using the ancient Greek example. South Carolina statesman John C. Calhoun, a product of the Scots-Irish Long Canes and a prime example of the South Carolina clique, turned to the ancient Greeks for his model of government. The underlying premise, Calhoun avowed, was the "realistic" assumption that within human society, a natural hierarchy of talents and abilities exists. In the Greek model, the inferiors serve their superiors, but those at the top of the hierarchy also have responsibilities to the well being of those at the bottom rung. *15*

Chapter Six

Hymnody and Psalmody

History is full of strange ironies, but none more strange than the chain of circumstances which led to Metrical Psalmody beginning as the favorite recreation of a gleeful Catholic court and ending as the exclusive "hall mark" of the severest form of Protestantism.

Within a short time after the inception of Psalmody in France, psalm singing became the badge of adherence to the Reformation. Among the Huguenots it was universal. Indeed, a contemporary writer dates the formation of the Huguenot Church by the introduction of this practice.

All that is most splendid and moving in the history of that church has some association with the psalms. Its soldiers sang them on the battlefield; its martyrs in the flames. So it was at Angers in 1556, as he was being alternately raised and lowered into the flames, that *Huguenot Jean Rabec continued to sing Psalm 79, his voice half-choked with blood,* until he perished to become an early martyr.

Hymnody and Psalmody

And it was while *a Protestant congregation was singing psalms* in the grange of Vassey in 1562, that Guise gave the signal for the massacre of the Huguenots, an act which finally provoked the Wars of Religion. The psalms became battle songs for the Huguenots. On the battlefield where Henry of Navarre's men fought were heard such chants as Psalms 76 or 188, or, above all, Theodore de Beze's version of Psalm 68. His Psaume de Batailles, "Que Dieu se monstre seulement," became the Marseillaise of the Huguenot Reformation.

Hymnody in the Reformed Church was rather seriously retarded for a number of years by the iconoclastic views of Calvin and Zwingli, even though one of the most beautiful and stirring of all Protestant hymns, *I Greet Thee Who My Sure Redeemer Art* was written by John Calvin.

These reformers frowned on church choirs, organs and every form of ecclesiastical art. Even hymns such as those used by the Lutherans were prohibited because they were productions of man. God could be worshiped in a worthy manner, according to Calvin's principles, only by hymns which were divinely inspired, namely the psalms of the Old Testament. This gave rise to a practice of "versifying" the psalms, or putting them into metrical form, in order that they might be sung. Calvin's insistence that there should be the strictest adherence to the original text often resulted in crude paraphrases.

The exclusive use of the psalms explains the development of so-called "psalmody" in the Reformed Church as over and against "hymnody" in the Lutheran Church.

From the ministers of Geneva and the council of Geneva we are told, "by the example of the ancient church and even the witness of St. Paul, it is good to sing in the congregation from the mouth and from the heart. The psalms can arouse us to lift up our hearts to God and move as to an ardor both to call upon and to exalt by praises the glory of His name."

They also recommended that, "children sing in a high distinct voice to which the people listen attentively, following with their hearts what is sung by mouth until little by little all will become accustomed to sing a song together."

In 1538 at Strasbourg, John Calvin took up his pastorate with the French émigré Congregation. It was here that he began his collection of psalms for French Huguenot singers. The translation into verse (French) and the setting to music (meter) were the chief causes of the Reformation in the Low Countries. In France the metrical version of the psalter set to popular music was one of the principal instruments in the success of the Reformed Church, the other being the invention of the printing press.

In Strasbourg, Calvin was impressed by the dignity and strength of the German melodies of Martin Luther which were simple, unadorned and direct. Unlike Calvin's, Luther's hymns and psalms have endured.

As the theologian of the French Huguenot Church at Strasbourg, John Calvin had the honor of editing the first printed edition of metrical psalms for church worship. Calvin came into possession of some metrical paraphrases of the psalms by the celebrated court poet Clement Marot, a very gifted and versatile genius, serving in the court of King Francis I.

Marot was not inclined to serious religion. However, his psalms became immensely popular with the French Huguenots and exerted a great influence in the struggle between the Protestants and the Roman Catholics.

Later, because of Catholic persecution, Marot fled to Geneva. Here he collaborated with Calvin in publishing the first edition of the famous Genevan Psalter in 1543.

Calvin's first Psalter, 1539, consisted of one psalm in prose and seventeen in verse, set to music. Twelve of these were by Marot and the remaining five were by Calvin himself. Calvin was no musician, but he was alive to the power of music to move the heart.

Further, the beauty of certain German tunes so struck Calvin's ear that he began composing metrical paraphrases of

Psalms 25 and 46. In addition, he put into meter the *Ten Commandments*, with the Kyrie Eleison as a refrain, the *Song of Simeon*, and the *Apostles Creed*. Calvin intended the *Song of Simeon, Psalm 113* and *Psalm 138* for the Communion and Post Communion Thanksgiving. *Psalm 25* and the *Ten Commandments* were sung after the Prayer of Confession.

In his later years, Calvin's colleague at Geneva was Theodore de Beze, the writer of the metrical version of *Psalm LXVIII,* (68), which was the battle song of the Huguenots (already mentioned). The work of translating the psalms into French verse was Beze's main contribution in Huguenot Psalmody.

Tunes with grave and noble type were needed, so Calvin brought from Paris a musician of rare capacity and distinction, Louis Bourgeois. Before his death in 1561, he composed a total of 115 tunes.

Bourgeois had difficult masters to serve. On one occasion he was thrown into prison for making alternations, afterwards approved, in some of the Strasbourg melodies. But he served his masters magnificently. He organized musical education, training the students and children so that by their singing, their elders might be instructed.

He wrote glorious tunes, among them were *Bourgeois, Commandments, Mon Dieu, Pret Moi, L'Oreille, Nunc Minittis, O Esca Viatorum, One Hundredth, Toulon, St. Michael, Old Hundred Twenty Fourth, Picardy and Rendez a Dieu.* Some of them, like Luther's were adaptations of popular airs, "purified and baptized into Christina seriousness."

Many of the best of them were such adaptations - no one can say which were his own. Harmonized editions were issued from the first, but were excluded from use in public worship. His efforts to introduce part singing into the church were steadily negated and, at last, in disgust, he left the city.

It is not known which melodies in the French Psalters were adopted or composed by Bourgeois. All were anonymous.

Some were secular and liturgical melodies. In the *Psalter of 1562* there were 125 melodies for which Bourgeois seems to have been responsible.

Claude Goudimel also deserves honor in connection with Genevan Psalmody, not as a writer of original tunes, but as harmonizer of those that were in use in contrapuntal style. *Nunc Dimittis* is one of them. Goudimel was one of the greatest of the sixteenth century tune masters. However, his adherence to the Huguenot cause cost him his life. When the massacre of St. Bartholomew occurred in 1572, he was one of the victims. He was beheaded in Lyon, after brutal treatment and his body thrown into the Rhone River.

Although discussion has dealt mostly with psalms and psalmody, another reference to hymnody should be included. While all of Germany during the latter half of the seventeenth century was singing the sublime lyrics of Paul Gerhardt, prince of Lutheran hymnists, the spirit of song was beginning to stir in the soul of another German poet, Joachim Neander. This man, whose name will always be remembered as the author of one of the most glorious hymns of praise of the Christian church, was the first German hymn writer produced by the Reformed or Calvinistic branch of the Protestant Church. The hymn by which we remember Neander is *Praise Ye the Lord, the Almighty*.

The Psalms were identified with the everyday life of the Huguenots. They were sung at meals in households like that of Coligny; to chant psalms meant in popular language, to turn Protestant. The meetings of persecuted Huguenots were summoned by the signing of a psalm; in woods and caverns, in dungeons, in exile in America, the Psalms still sounded from the lips of Huguenots. In the language of Psalms was commemorated the escape of those who fled from the country. To sing the Psalms of David, men left their native land and sought remote recesses of the earth.

It is quite probable that the *Genevan Psalter* was the first Protestant book of worship brought to American shores. In

1565, when French Huguenots sailed from their homeland to escape persecution and to form colonies in South Carolina and Florida, they found their spiritual consolation in singing psalm paraphrases of Clement Marot, de Beze, and Louis Bourgeois. This expedition, however, came to a tragic end the following year when all the members of the colony were massacred by Spaniards, not because they were French but *because they were Huguenots.*

During the executions of the Huguenots, the Catholic priests tried unsuccessfully to drown the thunder of Marot's Psalms with their Latin chants. But the words lacked the savage energy of the French Huguenots. *With charred lips the Huguenot sufferers raised the Psalms. Some whose tongues had been cut out uttered sounds in which, though barely articulate, bystanders recognized the familiar words of the Psalms.*

The metrical psalmody has for over four hundred years been connected with Protestant worship. The popularity of the Psalms extended to many lands - the Reformed Church in Germany and in Switzerland with its authoritative Psalter. They were translated into Dutch, Italian, Spanish, Bohemian, Polish, Latin, and even Hebrew - and exerted a very powerful influence on the shaping of the metrical Psalters of England and Scotland.

No Bach arose in France to do for the Genevan Psalter tunes as had been done for the Lutheran chorales, but the influence of Calvin prevailed over that of Luther and determined among other things the form of church song. The authority of Calvin's opinion and example found by the Huguenots was such that the usage of singing metrical Psalms as instituted at Geneva followed the spread Calvinistic doctrine through the world as a recognized feature of church order.

In Scotland, during the persecutions under Queen Mary, many of the leaders of the Reformation took refuge in Geneva - there in 1556 a collection of *One and Fiftie Psalms of David in Englishe Metre* was published. These were written by William Whittingham, brother-in-law of Calvin. When the exiles returned to Scotland after the death of Mary, they took the Psalm-singing practice with them. Knox and Whittingham and others of the Puritan party of exiles were deeply under Calvin's influence and were impressed by the psalm-singing he had set up in his little French Huguenot congregation. In preparing a service book for their own people to take the place of the Prayer Book, they were determined to introduce psalm-singing and so began the preparation of an English psalm book of which Calvin's French Psalter was the model.

To the Puritans the singing of psalms was the most sacred act of public worship. The old version gave in to a newer version of a rhetorical paraphrase which was much more in the nature of a hymn. There was more lyrical freedom than the old psalmody allowed, and in this respect it marked a decided step forward on the road to the introduction of hymns. The new version brought many fine new tunes into the field such as Croft's *St. Anne* and Croft's *Hanover* and *York* tunes, also. John Playford's *London New*, John Day's *St. Flavian* - found in the Scottish Psalter. *The Old Scots Psalm Tunes* are the strong, simple, dignified tunes from the old Scots Psalters, and these and others of the same spirit and model furnish the proper medium for the expression of the sentiment of the old metrical psalms. [1]

Hymnody and Psalmody

The music (GENEVA 130). The first French Psalter to be published was that edited by John Calvin, issued at Strassbourg in 1539. It contained this tune, set to Psalm 130. The same tune continued to be used for this Psalm in later editions of the French, English, and Scottish Psalters.

PSEAUME CXXX.

Prière ardente du fidéle dans le sentiment de ses péchez, & sa confiance en la grace de Dieu.

AU fort de ma détresse, Dans mes profonds ennuis, A toi seul je m'adresse, Et les jours, & les nuits. Grand Dieu, prête l'oreille A mes cris éclatans; Que ma voix te réveille, Seigneur, il en est tems.

2. Si ta rigueur extrême Nos péchez veut compter, O Majesté suprême, Qui pourra subsister? Mais ta clémence régne Sur ta sévérité; Et tu veux qu'on te craigne, Seigneur, pour ta bonté.

3. En Dieu je me console, Dans nes plus grands malheurs,

The Huguenots of New Bordeaux

French Psalter, 1539

PSEAUME LXVIII.

Pseaume prophétique du régne de Jésus-Christ, aprés un récit abrégé
des graces que Dieu avoit faites à l'ancien peuple.

Pf. 68.
se léve, & ses
ennemis se-
ront disper-
sé ceux
qui le haïssent
s'enfuiront de
devant lui.

Ue Dieu se montre seulement, Et l'on verra dans le moment, Abandonner la place: Le camp des ennemis é-pars, Epouvanté de toutes parts, Fuira devant sa face.

3 Tu les chas-
seras comme
la fumée est
chassée par le
vent; comme
la cire se fond
devant le feu,
ainsi les mé-
chans périront
devant Dieu.

On verra tout ce camp s'enfuir, Comme l'on voit s'éva-nouïr Une épaisse fumée; Comme la cire fond au feu, Ainsi des méchans, devant Dieu, La force est consumée.

4 Mais les ju-
stes se réjoui-
ront & s'égay-
eront de-
vant Dieu, &
tressailliront
de joye.

2. Mais, en présence du Seigneur, Les bons célébrent sa grandeur, Sa force & sa sagesse; Et dans les vifs tran-sports qu'ils ont, De voir les méchans qui s'en vont, Ils sautent d'allégresse. Justes, chantez tout d'une voix, Du

5 Chantez à
Dieu, psalmo-
diez son
Nom, exaltez
celui qui est
monté sur les
cieux; son
Nom est l'E-
ternel; & é-
gayez vous
en sa présence.

Dieu des Dieux, du Roi des Rois, La louange immortelle; Car sur la nue il est porté, Et, d'un nom plein de majesté, L'Eternel il s'appelle.

Hymnody and Psalmody

4 There the seers and fathers holy,
   There the prophets glorified,
   All their doubts and darkness ended,
   In the Light of Light abide.

There the saints, whose memories old
We in faithful hymns uphold,
Have forgot their bitter story
In the joy of Jesus' glory.

The Huguenots of New Bordeaux

In 1589, at the walls of Chateau d'Arques near Dieppe, the king, Henry of Navarre and his Huguenot followers were threatened and outnumbered by the Duc de Mayenne and his army of the League. 'Come, M. le Ministre', cried the king to Pastor Damour 'lift the psalm. It is full time.' Then, above the din of the marching armies, rose the words of Beze [Que Dieu se montre seulement] and swinging with the march of the Huguenot companies and the roll of cannon marked the time of the psalm — the sea fog cleared away and Henry's men in the castle could see to aim and defeat the Leaguers. The austere melody of the 68th Psalm was heard over the bat-

tlefield.

It is interesting to know the Psalter of 1731 was in the family of the Huguenot wife of Rev. William Tennett III who came to South Carolina. Also the Dutch Psalter of 1608 was used in New York and when the Huguenots fled there for refuge from persecution in France they were able to join their fellow Reformed Christians in singing the same Psalms although each in his own language.

The Huguenots of New Bordeaux

4 Thy bountiful care, what tongue can recite?
It breathes in the air; it shines in the light;
It streams from the hills; it descends to the plain,
And sweetly distils in the dew and the rain.

Chapter Seven

Huguenots in the Novel

During the time of the Revolutionary War, some ninety years after the Revocation of the Edict of Nantes, a number of Huguenots in South Carolina rose to prominence in public and military life. Henry Laurens, Francis Marion, Peter Horry, and Daniel Huger are some of the Huguenot names of South Carolinians who helped enrich the whole spirit of their new country at this period and fought to achieve its independence. Not surprisingly, then, several historical figures, along with fictional Huguenots, appear as characters in the Revolutionary War novels by South Carolina authors.

Of William Gilmore Sims' seven historical romances concerning the Revolution, six contain characters whose traits are sufficiently well delineated to warrant considering them as Huguenots. The series of novels shows the progress of the Revolution from the dark days of 1780 through the years immediately following the war.

About the same time that Sims was writing these romances, Mary Elizabeth Moragné of New Bordeaux won recognition in 1838 as the author of *The British Partizan*, a short novel of the Revolutionary War, in which her native Huguenot community is portrayed. The compelling and skillfully told romance is based on the lives of real persons against a historically-accurate background during the Revolutionary War. For her labors, the twenty-two year old author received a leather-bound set of Sir Walter Scott's novels. *The British Partizan* received high acclaim from Northern literary journals, the "Knickerbocker" declaring that it approached more nearly the style and genius of Sir Walter Scott than any novel that had yet been written this side of the Atlantic. To meet the demand for the story an edition was printed in book form, only a small portion of which, however, reached the public, the greater part of the edition having been destroyed while in sheets by the flood which inundated Augusta, Georgia in 1840. A publisher reprinted *The British Partizan* in 1864. The war time edition was bought by soldiers and civilians at seventy-five cents per copy.

The British Partizan is a tale of love and adventure with young Huguenot heroine Annette Bruyésant, and her father Pierre, who are both Patriots.

The British Partizan himself Ralph Cornet, joins the British forces, but when he learns of the atrocities committed by the Tories in the region, he regrets his allegiance to the British. However, he does not join the American forces. Instead he exiles himself from his former home. Ultimately, before Ralph leaves the vicinity of New Bordeaux forever, he and Annette are married by a French Protestant minister.

The important characters are all historical. The author describes the British Partizan, "when it comes to riding, running, wrestling, or fighting, there is not the man in this country whom Ralph Comet fears to face, hand to hand." Members of the author's mother's *Caine family* were the originals for the Cornets of the novel. *William Caine*, the British Partizan's elder

Mary Elizabeth Moragné

The Huguenots of New Bordeaux

brother Cornet in the story, had actually been killed by the Tories in the manner described.

Annette Bruyésant is described as a lovely, proud girl with a high sense of honor: "The soft exterior of the French girl covered a heart high and proud, which Ralph Cornet had in some measure formed in his own likeness - so naturally do proud hearts assimilate - but being more dispassionate, and with less ambition, she had clearer views of honor than he."

Annette Bruyésant's father Pierre Bruyésant, colorful and typically Huguenot, is patterned after the author's own *grandfather Pierre Moragné* who actually came to New Bordeaux as a refugee in 1764. Although Pierre Moragné had little on his small farm that could tempt the Tories, they took vengeance on him because of his outspoken remarks for the American patriots. They raided his place often and in one raid he was shot in the leg by the Tories who were attempting to steal his horses. Moragné survived the experience, but remained in a wakened condition for the rest of his life. His attachment to his little home was apparent when he requested that he be buried "under an elm tree near his cottage."

Ralph's slave friend Juba appears often: "Ralph stood by a tree outside the little enclosure ... whence he had a plain view of the scene, which made his blood to boil once more. There was his faithful Juba, hanging by the arms from a log which extended from a corner of the hut, and a man was still inflicting the punishment of the whip. Two other men stood by with drawn swords, laughing ... he examined the priming of the rifle and resting it slowly and steadily against the tree he took deliberate aim at the man who held the lash. With the report of the gun the man sprang at least three feet into the air and fell, like a lump of lead, with a groan."

General Andrew Pickens, Colonel John Dooly, British Major Patrick Ferguson, Hugh Bates and other Tories, appear under their own names. The author shifts minor historical incidents to fit her story, but her facts as a whole are accurate.

Huguenots in the Novel

In the novel, Mary Moragné employs authentic dialect for the speech of the elderly Huguenot Bruyésant. The French father spoke "in a ludicrous mixture of French and broken English," which Ralph Cornet had no trouble understanding because he had known the French language from infancy, owing to the prevalence among the French settlers in the New Bordeaux colony, who clung with fondness to this last relic of their native country.

Having been in the New World only about ten years, Bruyésant was no wealthy plantation owner but a small farmer with a comfortable little cottage. The old gentleman was grateful for the haven that South Carolina had given him, and he was "an avowed Republican." In fact, he "had expressed himself very boldly" in the cause of freedom. When Ralph joined the British, Pierre Bruyésant forbade his daughter to mention the youth's name in his presence again.

Earlier he had been most amiable to Ralph and had enjoyed joking with the young man about his interest in Annette. Once when Ralph complimented Mr. Bruyésant's daughter, the elderly Huguenot said, "Ma foi! ... she would be sorri veri much to dispute of dat, my son — ha! ha! Mais c'est egal; nevare mind, Ralph – de youg demoiselles know alway, quand elles sont jolies. N'est-ce pas, Annie!"

Practical and thrifty, Bruyésant dreaded to see the British soldiers come to his cottage time after time:

"Qui," replied the old man, "c'est bien vrais – dey come here wid de compaign of light horse – dey look so fine – mais! Dey scare de poor peoples half out of all dere sens. Dey drink tout le vin – dey sing, O mon Dieu! Que des British sont mechants!"

Yet he feared greatly that Whig sympathizers would not be safe from bodily harm and even warned Ralph, who he assumed was a through going Patriot like the rest of his family, to flee:

"O mon Dieu! Mon Dieu!" he exclaimed with clasped

hands, "nous sommes perdu-helas! I come here to find de peace, an' I shall find de trouble, Mais je sais mourir. Fuyer! My son, fuyer!"

The author's colorful depictions of local scenes in the setting further enhance the novel.

The Savannah River: "Who has seen and has not admired our beautiful Savannah? It is ever lovely, whether dashing in light ripples and foaming falls among the flowery precipices and purple rocks of Habersham, or whether spreading its broad bosom to the sea, still and wide, where the shadows of painted barges and smoking engines pass over it like the illusions of the enchanter's mirror."

Vienna, a small river town near New Bordeaux, is the setting for the home of her character Annette Bruyésant: " ... a smooth grass plain, and before him lay the little village of Vienna - houses rising in two rows from the river's bank. On the border of this plain, where it slopes gently down to the river, stood a little vine-covered cottage, the refuge of a French emigrant, one of the many who fled from intolerance in their own country, hoping to fine peace and the quiet worship of God in the shades of the great new world."[1]

In real life the author probably portrayed the home of Pierre La Brun, a Huguenot refugee. La Brun's daughter Mary was married to *Ralph* Roland in the cottage at Vienna by the author's beloved pastor Dr. Moses Waddel on a December evening during a snowy blizzard. The bride died on the first anniversary of her wedding. [2]

Fort Charlotte: "On the bank of the river, a little apart from Vienna ... a fort which was built for the defense of the early settlers against the Indians. Its walls were built of stone, and formed ten feet high, with port-holes and other appliances of stout resistance. Here Gen. Pickens supported his dependents, and old age and infancy flocked daily to the protecting care. But thanks to the cowardice of the tories, amd their successive defeats in open combat, this weak garrison was in no danger of attack."

Author Mary Elizabeth Moragné was born in New Bordeaux in 1816 and lived much of her life in Willington. She was a young woman of intellectual interests, keen observation, and the ability to express herself fluently and freely in prose. Besides *The British Partizan*, Moragné published *The Rencontre*, another story of the American Revolution, in 1841. Mr. Thompson, the editor of the "Augusta Mirror," remarked, "*The Rencontre* is of that class of literary production which we prize above all other orders of fiction. Illustrative as it is of our own history, descriptive of our own peculiar scenery, and abounding in sound reflections and truly elevated sentiment, we hold it worth volumes."

About this time there appeared in print some other pieces by Mary Moragné, both in prose and verse. One of the latter was called "Joseph, A Scripture Sketch, in Three Parts," comprising more than a thousands lines.

Near the end of year 1841, the periodical editor said in a review, "We have received the first part of a tale, entitled 'The Walsingham Family, or, A Mother's Ambition.' We are much pleased with it and do not hesitate to promise a rich treat." This was a domestic tale of some length, apparently designed to illustrate the folly and vanity of a worldly and ambitious mother. But, although the first six chapters were in the hands of the publisher, and the remainder ready for publication, it was entirely withdrawn by the author, notwithstanding the earnest solicitation of the editors because of growing conflict with her religion and opinions of her pastor who became her husband in 1842.

An important work of her life, never intended for publication, were her personal journals published in 1951 by Delle Mullen Craven as *The Neglected Thread*. The account of her early life during the years 1836-1842, beginning when she was nineteen, portrays a side of antebellum Southern life which, though it probably characterized the existence of the majority of Southerners, has so often been completely overshadowed by the tradition associated with the great plantations. For the most part, this back country region was not the South of pillared mansions but of plain, substantial frame houses, the homes of small plantation owners, of poor farm families and homes, of slave families, of country preachers and teachers. She carefully recorded life of this realm.

Upon her marriage to Rev. William H. Davis, pastor of Willington Presbyterian Church, Mary Moragné's life underwent a decided change. Her husband expressed his frank disapproval of her "tales," as he described the fiction she authored. Her interests were markedly altered. She experienced a great consciousness of sin, augmented by recurring periods of ill health and the difficulty in subduing a naturally haughty and overbearing disposition. Her family thought she was becoming over-religious. As a minister's wife, she broke off her literary connections and discontinued writing fiction, the art in which she was at her best and which would have brought her most fame and money. Nevertheless, she never gave up writing. She continued her journal all her life and contributed poems and numerous articles to newspapers, and to her church periodicals, *The Presbyterian of the South* and *The Christian Observer.* Among her published poems was a collection *Lays from the Sunny Lands,* published fifty years after *The British Partizan.*

Following her husband's death, Mary Elizabeth Moragné remained head of her family until her death at age eighty-seven, a proud, versatile, keen-minded woman, who had outlived not only her generation, but also the very social and economic structure of her time. [3]

Notes

Introduction
1. Davis, Dr. Nora M., Unpublished Papers
    Hirsch, Arthur H., *The Huguenots of Colonial South Carolina,* Columbia, 1999
    Huguenot Society of South Carolina, 1920 Transactions, Charleston

Chapter One, Religious Wars and Diaspora
1. Edmonds, Bobby F., *The Making of McCormick County,* p. 50-82, McCormick
    Hillhouse, Albert M., *Pierre Gibert, French Huguenot,* p. 1-65, Danville, 1977
    Hirsch, *Ibid.*
    Huguenot Society, 1920 Transactions
    McGrath, Alister E., *A Life of John Calvin,* p. 1-19, Oxford, 1990
    Van Ruymbeke, Bertrand, Randy J. Sparks, *Memory and Identity,* Columbia, 2003
2. Frieda, Leonie, *Catherine de Medici,* p. 267-272, New York, 2003
3. Hillhouse, *Ibid.*
    Hirsch, *Ibid.*
    Van Ruymbeke, *Ibid.*

Chapter Two, The Pastor of the Desert
1. Edmonds, *Ibid.*
    Davis Papers
    Hillhouse, *Ibid.*
    Peace, Jane H. and William H., *A Family of Women,*

p. 9-12, Chapel Hill, 1999

Chapter Three, The Long Voyage
1. Davis Papers
   Moragné, Pierre, Journal
2. Moragné, William C., Address, November 15, 1854
3. Moragné Journal
4. Davis Papers
5. South-Carolina Historical Society, Collections,
   Volume II, Charleston, 1858
6. Davis Papers
   Moragné Journal
7. Fraser, Jr., Walter J., *Charleston! Charleston!* p. 3-97,
   Columbia, 1989
8. Davis Papers

Chapter Four, New Bordeaux Colony Founded
1. Davis Papers
2. Edmonds, p. 127
3. Davis Papers
   Hart, John S., *The Female Prose Writers of America*,
   p. 455, 456, Philadelphia, 1870
   Hirsch, p. 202-207
4. Davis Papers
5. Nova Scotia web page
6. Sandra Delashaw Warden, Unpublished Manuscript
7. Davis Papers
   Hirsch, p. 202-207
8. Davis Papers
   Warden Manuscript
9. Ludlum, David M., *Early American Winters*,
   p. 143-144, Boston, 1966
   Ludlum, David M., *The Weather Factor*, p. 11-13, Boston,
   1984
10. Colonial Records

Notes

Davis Papers
11. Medicine, Article by Janet J. Wong, MD, June 28, 2005
12. Colonial Records
Davis Papers
13. Colonial Records
Davis Papers
Hirsch
14. Colonial Records
Davis Papers
15. Colonial Records
Davis Papers
Hirsch
16. Colonial Records
Davis Papers
17. Davis Papers
William C. Moragné, Address, November 15, 1854
18. *Ibid.*
19. Davis Papers

Chapter Five, Assimilation
1. Davis Papers
Wessely, J. E., *Junior Classic French Dictionary*, Chicago, 1947
2. Pease, Jane H. And William H., *A Family of Women,* p. 10-12, Chapel Hill, 1999
3. Gibert, Anne C., *Pierre Gibert, Esq., The Devoted Huguenot,* p. 73, Columbia, 1976
4. Davis Papers
Warden Manuscript
5. Carson, James Petigru, *Life, Letters and Speeches of James Louis Petigru,* p. 18, Washington, 1920
6. Gibert, p. 56
7. Craven, Delle Mullen, *The Neglected Thread,* p. xxxiii, Columbia, 1951
8. Davis Papers

9. Gibert
10. Davis Papers
11. Edmonds, *The Making*
    Davis Papers
12. Hart, p. 456, 457
13. Moragné Address
    Edmonds, *Land of Cotton*
14. Edmonds, Land of Cotton
    Ware, Lowry, *Slave Holders of Abbeville District, 1790-1860,* p. 1-8
15. Ware, *Ibid.*
    Sass, Herbert Ravenel, *Look Back to Glory,* p. 18, Charleston, 2005

Chapter Six, Hymnody and Psalmody
1. Singleton, Lucy Ann Blanchard, *Huguenot Hymnody and Psalmody,* p. 1-25, 1983

Chapter Seven, Huguenots in the Novel
1. Anderson, Mary Crow, *The Huguenot in the South Carolina Novel,* unpublished thesis, 1966
   Hart, p. 453-457
2. *The Abbeville Medium,* March 24, 1898
3. Anderson, Ibid
   Hart, Ibid
   Craven, p. xxii-xxxviii

Bibliography

Anderson, Mary Crow, *The Huguenot in the South Carolina Novel*, Ann Arbor, 1966
Bass, Robert D., *Ninety Six*, Lexington, 1978
Davis, Dr. Nora M., Nora M. Davis Papers, unpublished
Davis, Dr. Nora M. *A Register of Marriages by Moses Waddel, 1795-1836*, Columbia, 1943
Edmonds, Bobby F., *The Making of McCormick County*, McCormick, 1999
Edmonds, Bobby F., *McCormick County Land of Cotton*, McCormick, 2001
Fraser, Jr., Walter J., *Charleston! Charleston!*, Columbia, 1989
Frieda, Leonie, *Catherine de Medici*, New York, 2003
Gibert, Anne C., *Pierre Gibert, Esq., The Devoted Huguenot*, Columbia, 1976
Golden, R. M., *The Huguenot Connection: The Edict of Nantes*, Dordrecht, 1988
Hart, John S., *The Female Prose Writers of America*, Philadelphia, 1870
Hillhouse, Albert M., *Pierre Gibert, French Huguenot*, Danville, 1977
Howard, Nell H., and Bessie W. Quinn, *Moragnes in America*, Birmingham, 1971
Howe, George, *History of the Presbyterian Church, Vol. I*, Columbia, 1870
Hirsch, Arthur H., *The Huguenots of South Carolina*, Columbia, 1999
Huguenot Society of SC, Transactions, Charleston, 1920, 1937, 1951
Library of Congress, No. 121, Petition of Louis Dumesnil de

St. Pierre to Council
Ludlum, David M., *Early American Hurricanes,* Boston, 1963
Ludlum, David M., *Early American Winters*, Boston, 1966
Ludlum, David M., *The Weather Factor*, Boston, 1984
McGrath, Alister E., *A Life of John Calvin,* Oxford, 1990
Meriwether, Robert L., *The Expansion of South Carolina*, Kingsport, 1940
Moragne, W. C., 90th Anniversary Address on the Arrival of the French Huguenots, November 15, 1854
Moragne, Mary Elizabeth, *The British Partizan*, Macon, 1864
Pease, Jane H. and William H., *A Family of Women, The Carolina Petigrus*, Chapel Hill, 1999
Ruymbeke, Bertrand Van and Randy J. Sparks, *Memory and Identity*: The Huguenots in France, Columbia, 2003
Singleton, Lucy Ann Blanchard, *Huguenot Hymnody and Psalmody*, The National Huguenot Society, 1983
South-Carolina Historical Society, Collections, Volume II, Charleston, 1858
Spitz, Lewis W., *The Protestant Reformation, 1517-1559,* New York, 1985
Sutherland, N. M., *The Huguenot Struggle for Recognition*, New Haven, 1980
The South-Carolina Gazette, February 8-15, 1768
United States Census
Warden, Sandra Delashaw, unpublished manuscript
Ware, Lowry, *Slave Holders of Abbeville District*
Wessely, J. E., *French Dictionary*, Chicago, 1947

Index

Aime, Eliz. Bien, 31
Alegresse, Jeanne, 31
Alexandre, Susanne, 31
Allen, Amanda Rachel, 76
Amnieu, Marthe, 41
Anger, Jacob, 52
Anthony, Jean, 40
Antony, Jean, 29
Archbishop Stecker, 20
Armagnieu, Marthe, 30
Audebert, Jean, 40, 67
Audibert, Jean, 28
Audouin, Andre, 27
Augustin, Laurant, 52
Bach, Jacob, 46
Bach, Peter, 46
Barbier, Pierre, 30
Barchinger, Johann, 64
Barksdale, Mary, 76
Barnier, Claude, 51
Bartram, William, 62
Basson, Nicholas, 40
Basson, Nichs., 30
Bates, Hugh, 102
Baylard, Jacob, 28, 41, 67
Bayle, Marie Seyral, 50
Bayle, Francois, 28
Bayle, Marie, 40
Bayle, Francis, 40
Bayle, Jean, 50
Bayle, Cecile, 31, 40, 50
Bayle, Pierre, 28, 40
Beach Island, 33
Beard, Philip, 41

Beattie, Anne, 77
Beekler, Nicholas, 46
Beillard, Jean Pierre, 30
Beinayme, Anne Beraud, 39
Bellefaye, Anne, 31
Bellefaye, Jean, 29, 39
Bellier, Jean Pierre, 40
Bellot, Jean, 39
Bellot, Pierre, 51, 67
Bellot, Helie, 51
Bellote, Marie Madelaine, 31
Bellote, Me. Judith, 31
Bellotte, Pierre Elie, 29
Bellotte, Jean, 29
Bellotte, Jean Arnaud, 29
Belot, Marie Magdale, 40
Belot, Jacob, 7
Belot, Pierre Elie, 39
Belotte, Jean, 67
Beraud, Marie, 30
Beraud, Jean, 52
Beraud, Matthew, 39
Beraud, Anne, 30, 31
Beraud, Mathew, 41
Beraud, Jean du Conton, 41
Béraud, Matthew, 67
Bereau, Matthieu, 27
Bereau, Matthieu, 27
Billaud, Antoine, 29
Billaw, Antoine, 40
Blanchet, Jean Pierre, 51
Bereau, Jean, 27
Blanchet, Jeanne, 31
Bollomay, Samuel, 29

Bonneau, Jean, 28
Bonneaud, Jeanne, 31
Bordajeau, Colas, 29, 39
Bordajeau, Marie, 31
Bordajeau, Jeanne, 31
Bordajeau, Pierre, 29, 67
Bouchelle, Amanda, 77
Bordajeau, Jean, 29
Bouchelon, Joseph, 39
Bouchilion, Jean, 40
Bouchillon, James Leonard, 77
Bouchillon, Joseph, 28, 67-69
Bouchillon, Jean, 28
Bouchineau, Charles, 67
Bouchonau, Marie, 30
Bouchonaud, Nic., 29
Bouchonaud, Charles, 29
Bouchonneau, Anne Courneau, 39
Bouchonneau, Charles, 40
Bouchonneau, Nicholas, 40
Boudet, Pierre, 21
Bouigue, Barthelemy, 27
Boulonge, James Sezor, 60
Bourgeois, Louis, 89
Boutiton, Jean, 28, 30
Boutiton, Jacque, 27, 39
Boutiton, Pierre, 20, 30, 39, 44, 46, 52, 78, 79
Boyan, Pierre, 51
Boyer, Pierre, 30
Boyer, Jean, 28
Branton, Francois, 30
Breazeal, Archibald, 76
Breazeal, Nancy, 76
Brewer, Theodore, 64
Brieau, Jean, 28
Britt, Elizabeth Roberson, 77
Britt, Charles, 55

Bryan, Delilah, 76
Buffalo Baptist Church, 81
Bull, Lt. Gov. William, 43, 47, 60, 61, 65, 66, 78, 79
Bute, Lord, 20
Caine, William, 100
Caine, Margaret Blanton, 76
Calder, Robert, 67
Calhoun, James, 76
Calhoun, John C., 85
Calhoun, Patrick, 43-48
Calvin, John, 2-15, 87, 88
Cape Sable Island, 55
Caris, Jeanne, 31
Carrol, Ellis, 76
Cartau, Jean, 40
Castan, Jean, 29
Castine, Jean, 67
Castle, Robert, 59
Catherine de Medici, 10, 11
Cawsey, Capt. Wm., 56-59
Chabar, Claude, 51
Chamberland, Jean, 67
Chamberland, Jacques, 51
Chamberland, John, 76
Chardavoine, Jacob, 27
Chareau, Pierre, 29
Charles Town, 37, 38
Charles IX, 10, 11
Charleston, 1
Chauvet, Claude, 51
Chauvet, Paul, 51
Chenton, Pierre, 51
Cherokee Indians, 47, 66, 67
Chuseau, Pierre, 28
Clay, John, 76
Cluzzeau, Pierre, 40
Commer, Pierre, 52
Cook, Rebekah, 76

Index

Cor, Mathias, 64
Cornwallis, Lord Edward, 54
Corrteiz, Pierre, 18
Coureau, Anne, 30
Court, Antoine, 18
Covin, Lazarus, 67
Covin, Peter, 76
Covin, Susan, 76
Covin, Elizabeth, 76
Craven, Delle Mullen, 105
Creek Indians, 47
d'Etaples, Lefevre, 2
Dabbs, Jesse, 76
David, Jean, 67
Davis, William Hervey, 76, 106
Davis, James, 46
de Coligny, Admiral Gaspard, 10, 11
de Birague, René, 11
de Villegagnon, Doran, 10
de la Gay, 41
de Berquin, Louis, 8
de Beze, Theodore, 89
de Goutrespac, M., 21
De la Chaux, Jacob, 55, 59,
De Martile, Abram, 59
De la Mare, Marie, 32
De la Chaux, James, 55
De la Chaux, Jeanne Loup, 55
De la Chaux, Jean Nicolas, 55
De la Chaux, Sara Britt, 55
De Laune, Jean Baptiste, 39
Deason, Elizabeth, 59
Delamore, John, 61
Delashaw, Catherine, 76
Delaunnay, Marie, 32
Delonay, Jn. Bte., 29
Delonay, Jacques, 29

Delonay, Antonio, 29
Depre, Jean LeDue, 59
Dickson, Sarah, 77
Dillashaw, Elizabeth, 76
Dillashaw, Jacob, 76
Dilleshaw, Peter, 76
Don, Jean, 40
Dooly, John, 102
Don, Pre Pierre, 27
Dorothea, Anna, 59
Drayer, Heinrich, 59
Dron, Jean, 51
Du Vall, Jean, 59
Ducerqueil, F. LeRoy, 67
Due, Daniel, 27, 40
Dugas, Pierre, 20
Due, Capt., 44, 46
Duke of Nevers, 11
Duke of Anjou, 11
Dumas, Pierre, 28
Dupuis, Jean, 28
Dupuy, Jean, 41
Earl of Hillsborough, 32, 33, 43, 65
Engevine, Pierre, 75
Enharding, Rosina, 65
Enharding, Barbara, 65
Eymery, Jean, 40
Eymery, Jean, 30
Faber, John, 8
Farastau, Antoine, 29
Faveraud, Jean, 28
Favereau, Marie, 31
Favereau, Etienne, 28
Favereau, Francoise, 32
Ferasteau, Marie, 31
Ferasteau, Marie, 31
Ferguson, Major Patrick, 102

Festal, Mathieu, 29
Forrester, Elizabeth, 59
Fort Lyttleton, 41
Fort Charlotte, 66, 104
Fort Engevin, 68
Fort Cowen, 68
Fort Boone, 50
Fort Moore, 33
French Santee, 1
Fresille, Marie, 31
Fresille, Judith, 31
Fresille, Jean, 39
Fresille, Susanne, 31
Frick, Johann Gerlogh, 59
Frisille, Jean, 27
Gabau, Marie Farasteau, 39
Gabeau, Antoine, 29, 67
Gaillard, Peter, 64
Gaillard, Claude, 64
Garrineau, Pierre, 40
Garrineau, Pierre, 67
Garrineau, Pre., 30
Gasper, Heinrich, 59
Gautier, Jean Baptiste, 39
Gautier, Theodore, 29
Gautier, Jean Bte., 29
Gautier, N., 31
Gay, Theodore, 40
Gerard, Francis, 30
Gereau, Jacques, 28
Gerhardt, Paul, 90
Gibert, Drusilla, 76
Gibert, Elizabeth Bienamè, 76
Gibert, Harriet, 76
Gibert, Dr. Joseph, 76
Gibert, Joseph, 75, 76
Gibert, Jeanne, 75, 76
Gibert, Pierre, 67, 77, 78, 80

Gibert, Louise, 75, 76
Gibert, Stephen, 76
Gibert, Lucy, 76
Gibert, Jean Louis, 2, 18-24, 34, 39, 52-54
Gognet, Ledie, 31
Goguett, Thomas, 59
Gollin, Pierre, 27
Gollin, Jeanne, 31
Goose Creek, 1
Gottier, Jean, 65
Goudimel, Claude, 90
Graham, Mary Catherine, 76
Gransar, Jean Jacques, 51
Gregoire, Eliz., 30
Gros, Francois, 28, 40
Grumblack, Thomas, 46
Guay, Theodore, 29
Guillebeau, André, 28, 40, 67
Guillebeau, Lazarus, 77
Guilliame, Amel, 32
Halifax, 54
Harbuck, John, 76
Heller, Francis, 60
Henry of Navarre, 87
Henry II, 2
Henry of Guise, 11
Herport, Antne., 30
Heynard, Archibald, 59
Hillhouse, Joseph, 76,
Holmes, Hogden, 84
Hook, Wilhelm, 64
Hopewell Church, 69, 80
Horry, Peter, 99
Hotman, François, 11
Houser, Andrew, 46
Houston, William, 76
Huger, Daniel, 99

Index

Hugues, Ann, 59
Husson, Jn. Louis, 30
Husson, Marie, 32
Jacob, Daniel, 29
Jacob, Abram, 29, 39
Jacob, Marie Judith, 32
Jager, Heinrich, 64
Jeachin, Stephen, 65
Jenkinson, Charles, 33
Jennerett, Daniel Louis, 39
Joly, Susanne Isabeau, 32
Kennedy, Benjamin, 76
King George III, 21, 24, 33, 81, 82
La Faye, Jacques, 29
La Faye, Jean, 29
La Lande, Francis, 59
La Fille ,Nicholas, 64
Labbe, Antoine Joseph, 68
Labbe, Joseph, 41
Labbe, Ant. Jos., 30
Labrousse, Marie, 31
Labrousse, Jacques, 28
Labrousse, Etienne, 28
Labrousse, N., 30
Labruese, Jacque, 39
Lafonde, Susanne, 31
Langel, Pierre, 30
Langel, Anne, 31
Langel, Jacob, 28
Langel, Jacques, 28
Langel, Denis, 28
Langell, Jacque, 39, 41
Langell, Pierre, 41
Lartege, Lour Loram, 64
Lartigue, Pierre, 28
Latou, Anne, 41
Latou, Susanna, 41

Latour, Anne, 30
Latour, Suzanne, 30
Laurens, Henry, 99
Lazenby, Catherine, 76
Le Riche, Pierre, 51
Le Fevre, Jeanne, 32
Le Gros, Jacques, 51
Lee, Stephen, 76
Lefaye, Jean, 39
Leoron, Lt., 44, 46
Leoron, Pierre, 40
LeQuo, Magdeline, 60
LeRoy, Jean, 77
LeRoy, Peter, 77
LeRoy, Peter Michl., 59
Lespine, Anne, 30
Levoilett, Ensign, 44, 46
Levrier, Rev. Peter, 79
Liberty M. H., 80, 81
Lievre, Jeanne, 31
Lioron, Pierre, 27
Lisbon, 84, 85
Little River, 43
Locke, John, 4
Long Cane Creek, 43
Lord Hardwicke, 20
Lord Charles Montagu, 58, 66
Lord Halifax, 32
Louis XIV, 12, 13
Luther, Martin, 3, 8
Maginier, Marie, 31
Majendie, Rev., 20
Manigault, Gabriel, 52, 53
Mann, Samuel, 76
Marechal, Louis, 52
Marion, Francis, 99
Marot, Clement, 88
Marshal de Tavannes, 11

Martin, Leonard, 76
Martin, John, 76
Martin, Sarah, 76
Masle, Jean Jacques, 65
McLinton, Robert, 76
McNutt, 33, 34
Mecklin, Rev. Robert, 80
Metager, Gear Lad, 64
Miolett, Jean, 65
Moragné, William Caine, 83
Moragné, Francis, 76
Moragné, Pierre, 25, 26, 27, 34-37, 41, 50, 67, 68, 103
Moragné, Pierre Francis, 76
Moragné, Jr., Pierre, 67, 81
Moragné, Isaac, 76
Moragné, Mary Elizabeth, 49, 76, 77, 82, 83, 100-106
Morin, Anne Julne., 32
Mt. Tabor Meth. Church, 81
Muyssen, Rev., 20
Neander, Joachim, 90
New Bordeaux, 43-73
Nicholas, Pierre, 39
Nicholas, Jn. Pre., 30
Nino, Paul, 27
Noble, Jean Jacques, 68
Orange Hill, 61
Orange Quarter, 1
Palmer, Marcella, 77
Parris Island, 41
Paulet, Jacques, 52
Pavennes, Jacques, 8
Paw, Abraham, 59
Perkins, George, 34-37
Petersburg, 69, 84, 85
Petit, Jn. Bte., 29
Petit, Benjamin, 67
Petite, Jean Baptiste, 39
Pettigrew, William, 77

Pettigrew, Louise, 77
Pettigrew, Sarah, 76
Pfaff, Wilhelm, 64
Pfeiffer, Jacole, 64
Pickens, Andrew, 102
Pieron, Pierre, 41
Piron, Pre. Nicholas, 30
Pitt, Mr., 20
Plisson, Jean, 52
Poitbin, Matthieu, 52
Poitevin, Jn. Fs., 30
Poitevin, Ane. Julne., 32
Poitevin, Jn. Fs., 30
Port Royal, 41
Pownall, J., 33
Priolot, Jean, 28, 40
Prouillac, Francois, 28, 40
Purrysburgh, 1, 3
Quate, Marie, 31
Rabec, Jean, 86
Reigne, Pierre, 29, 39
Renateau, Francoise, 31
Renond, Pierre, 28
Reparon, Marie, 32
Revere, Laurens, 59
Ribault, Jean, 10
Roger, Jean, 39
Roger, Pierre, 27, 40
Roger, Justice, 46
Roger, Marie, 40
Roger, Jeremiah, 40
Rogers, Sally, 76
Roger, Pierre, 67, 68
Roger, Jean, 27
Roger, Marte., 30
Rogers, Eliza, 76
Rogers, Robert, 59
Rolland, Joseph, 28
Rolland, Pierre, 28, 40
Roquemore, Jean, 28

Index

Roquemore, Pre, 28
Roquemore, Pierre Ayne, 39
Roquemore, Marie, 31
Roudier, Jeanne, 30
Roquemore, Anne, 40
Roquemore, Jean Pierre, 40
Roquemore, Susanna, 40
Roquemore, Pierre, 28
Rougimont, Arnuldus, 64
Roujon, Marie, 31
Roulland, Joseph, 52
Royan, France, 24
Ruppel, Martif, 64
Sacboville, Francoise, 31
Saint John's Berkeley, 1
Saller, Will, 64
Salleri, Louis, 51
Savannah River, 104
Scervante, Jean, 41
Scurvy, 55, 58
Seguin, Jeanne, 31
Seiral, Marie, 31
Shields, William P., 77
Shirley, Delilah America, 77
Shultz, Heinrich Abraham, 64
Sims, William Gilmore, 99
Slater, Johann Bennet, 64
Smith, Michael, 46
Smith, John, 66
Smith family, Aaron, 66
Sneider, Johann, 65
Springer, Rev. John, 80
St. Pierre, Marie, 56
St. Pierre, Jean Louis du Mesnil de, 54-68
St. Pierre, Henrietta, 56
Steifel, Johann, 59
Steinoch, Samuel, 65
Stuart, John, 66
Sudre, Pierre, 67

Sudze, Pierre, 41
Summerman, Martin, 46
Sundre, Pierre, 29
Tanasteau, Anthoine, 40
Taylor, Jane, 76
Terry, Jane, 76
Tessandier, Marguerite, 30
Testall, Matthiew, 41
Thomas, Etienne, 30
Thomas, Marie, 32
Thomas, Marie, 41
Thomson, James, 76
Tobert, Georg, 65
Touzeau, Jacques, 27
Vaillant, Pierre, 51
Vallae, Jacque, 41
Verdiere, Marie, 31
Vidau, Jean, 28
Vidau, Louis, 28
Vienna, 69, 84, 85, 104
Vilke, Marie, 32
Villaret, Pierre, 52
Villaret, Louis, 27
Villaret, Jean Villaret, 27
Villaret, Louis, 30
Villerett, Louis, 40
Waddel, Moses, 69, 70, 80, 81
Wagnon, Andre, 29
Watson, Dorcas Watson, 76
Weeks, Jane, 76
Whitney, Eli, 84
Whittingham, William, 91
Wilks, George, 68
William, Anny, 41
Williamson, Major, 66
Willingham, Johann, 64
Willington Pres. Ch., 81